This Is the Life

Mindfulness, Finding Grace, and the Power of the Present Moment

TERRY HERSHEY

franciscan
media
Cincinnati, Ohio

Cover and book design by Mark Sullivan

ISBN 978-1-63253-278-7

Published by Franciscan Media
28 W. Liberty St.
Cincinnati, OH 45202
www.FranciscanMedia.org

Printed in the United States of America.
Printed on acid-free paper.
19 20 21 22 23   5 4 3 2 1

This book is dedicated to my friend Ed's boat, The Promise.

● ● ● ● ●

And to Ed Kilbourne and Kent Kilbourne,
my friends who made my dance with manatees possible.

Contents

SECTION ONE

· · · · ·

We Are Born to Savor

Chapter One

Dancing with Manatees

I am convinced that it is not the fear of death, of our lives ending, that haunts our sleep so much as the fear that as far as the world is concerned, we might as well never have lived. —HAROLD KUSHNER

If you must look back, do so forgivingly. If you must look forward, do so prayerfully. However, the wisest thing you can do is be present in the present...gratefully. —MAYA ANGELOU

You never know what you're going to encounter en route. [So, now] I don't miss a thing. I touch everything. —ANDY MERRIFIELD

They tell us to live one day at a time—as if we had a choice. Two, three days at a time? Of course, all of us live one day at a time. Some of us are just more aware of it. —TOM BRAZAITIS

Not that long ago, I danced with manatees. Lord have mercy, it was good. I was in Manasota Key, Florida, my annual May gathering with my friends of thirty-five years. We swap stories and talk about the way the world would be if we were in charge. On the Intracoastal Waterway, near a congregation of mangrove trees, we anchor the boat and spend an afternoon floating, buoyed in the water, a treat for those of us who are escaping winter's chill. The sky is dyed hope-blue, and egrets pose graceful and elegant in the mangroves.

3

Manatees are curious and unafraid of humans. They are gentle, docile, and friendly. So, without announcement, they swim near and around you, to check out the visitors to their world. One manatee swam under my feet, literally lifting me up, as if to welcome me. Oh my. This is a first for me. I had heard stories. And yet, no mental framing prepares you. I do know this; in that moment, as my laughter echoes in the mangrove trees, as the cares of my day dissipate, I am fully awake and fully alive. My senses are grounded to *this* sacrament. *This* present moment. *This* gift. *This* clarity. *This* permission to savor life now goes with me into my day.

So, I wonder, why are there too many days when I miss the gift?

In letters written in 1740, Jean-Pierre de Caussade (ordained member of the Society of Jesus) wrote about the sacrament of the present moment. We are invited to choose to live each day as a sacrament (as a gift), enabling us to see, to hear, to taste, and to touch grace—the goodness of God's presence in our world. We need to bring this sacrament back and allow it to be front and center in our lives. I'm pretty sure that St. Francis would agree. Franciscan spirituality is an incarnational earthy spirituality. Put simply: God is close, never far away.

I live on an island in the Pacific Northwest, a long way from manatees, but that doesn't stop me from dancing with them. Every day. If only in my mind. "Dancing with manatees" is my shibboleth, inviting me to live and savor the sacrament of the present. And I invite you to do the same.

Whenever we broach the subject of spirituality or spiritual growth or emotional well-being, our knee-jerk petition is predictable, "Please tell us how." After all, there must be a list, right?

Which takes my mind to a story.

My son Zach is six, we are taking a break, sitting on the bench in front of Bob's Bakery (Bob's is Vashon Island's morning gathering spot). We're having Cinnamon Twists. They are decadently yummy, and make me forget my need to be useful. The bench is made from a trunk of an old downed log, its seat now worn from years of time and use. Zach and I watch the Vashon traffic — "traffic" in a poetic license sort of way — go by. And Zach, his mouth full of half a Twist, says, "Dad, this is the life."

"Life is full of beauty. Notice it," Ashley Smith writes. "Notice the bumble bee, the small child, and the smiling faces. Smell the rain, and feel the wind. Live your life to the fullest potential, and fight for your dreams."

Really, Terry, this is your list?

Do you remember the Road to Emmaus story? After the resurrection, Jesus joins two disciples walking a pathway. They are crestfallen that, after his death, Jesus has vanished; they are hoping for clarification about their sorrow. "Please explain," they say to Jesus. They ask questions. And Jesus tells them stories. Except they don't realize it is Jesus.

It was after walking, and after the "explanation," when Jesus sits down to break bread and to eat with them that their eyes opened. And they see. After Jesus departs, they say to one another, "Did not our hearts burn within us?" The gift, the clarity, the permission to see and to savor now accompanies them into their day.

Sadly, my religious upbringing didn't teach me about savoring and loving *this* life. And my church most certainly didn't teach me to dance with manatees. (Not to mention that in our lexicon, dancing was most assuredly a sin.) Raised Baptist in Southern Michigan, I was taught to value my faith. To live as if it mattered. And my life did matter, as a belief. As a creed. Well, more like a security card. Like a hall pass for eternity.

I was raised in a tradition that sang lustily, "This world is not my home, I'm just a-passing through." Saving up credits for heaven's golden streets and all that. I was asked persistently by concerned adult church members, "If you were to die tonight, do you know if you would spend eternity in heaven?" I'll give you a hint, you'd want to answer "Yes" because it saved consternation, and a mini-sermon.

As an adult, I realize now, looking back, that no one ever asked me, "If you were to live today, how would you savor this gift you've been given?" "If you were to live today, how would you embrace this sacrament of the present moment?" "If you were to live today, tell me, would you dance with manatees?"

Here's what I do now know: When we stop the noise, the distraction, the compulsion to perform, the fear of rejection, we make (meaning allow) space to practice this "new" sacrament.

The first-grade class assignment: to name the seven wonders of the world. Each student compiles a list, and shares that list, aloud, with the class. There is ardent interaction as the students call out entries from their lists: the Pyramids, the Empire State Building, the Amazon River, Yellowstone National Park, the Grand Canyon, the Taj Mahal and the list goes on. The teacher serves the role of cheerleader, "Class, these are great answers. Well done!"

One girl sits silent. She is asked about her list. She says, "I don't think I understand the assignment."

"Why?"

"I don't have any of the right answers," she tells the teacher.

"Well, why don't you tell us what you wrote on your paper, and we'll help you?" the teacher encourages her.

"OK," says the little girl, "I think the seven wonders of the world are to see, to hear, to taste, to touch, to smell, to love, to belong."

Somewhere along the way, we have buried this little girl's wisdom.

With these seven wonders, we make the choice to be open, available, curious and willing to be surprised by joy. We know there is power in the word *enough*. We carry this capacity to honor the present into every encounter and relationship, meaning that we honor the dignity that is reflected by God's goodness and grace. Every encounter, every relationship, is a place to include, invite mercy, encourage, receive, heal, reconcile, repair, say thank you, pray, celebrate, refuel, and restore.

A seminary student body participated in a day of recollection and reflection. As the seminary president introduced the guest retreat leader—on a beautiful Saturday morning in spring—he apologized to the seminarians, "I'm very sorry for the distraction and the noise."

This Saturday—on the seminary grounds sports field—happened to be youth soccer day. It seems that the president had forgotten to arrange for the local youth soccer program to play their games elsewhere on the day of the retreat. Hundreds of children were on the seminary grounds, and the sounds of play and laughter could easily be heard, echoing and reverberating inside the lecture hall.

But when the retreat leader stood up to begin his first talk of the day, he said, "I think it's wonderful that the children are here with us this morning. I will not have done my job if you aren't able to have a good retreat while you see and hear the sights and sounds of children playing on our soccer fields today."

It sounds good, doesn't it? I'm just not sure how easy it is to practice.

I received a call about a job, asking if I would I be willing to give a motivational talk to a group of health-care professionals. The caller explained, "Our people are very busy. Their life can be crazy. They juggle and multitask. So, your power of pause message sounds just right."

"Thank you," I tell her.

"But," she asks (and this is always the caveat), "How do we actually practice it? The pause part? How do we make this work in real life? In the real world?"

That is the issue, isn't it? Life tilts, and turns left when we least expect it. And we want someone to give us the answers. Or to try to balance it all. We want someone to give us the "how." And, on a day when we pray for motivation, reassurance, and illumination, we are told that it is enough to take delight in the play and laughter—the noise—of children, and the savoring of a Cinnamon Twist.

Yes. It is enough.

Living intentionally and fully alive—from a place of groundedness, being at home in our own skin—is not a technique. Nor is it a kind of mental Rubik's cube, to be solved. There is no list. But if we demand one, chances are, we pass this life by—the exquisite, the messy, the enchanting, the wondrous, the delightful, the untidy—on our way to someplace we think we ought to be.

On our journey together in this book, we will be learning new paradigms. There is meaning—consequence, value, import—only when what we believe or practice touches *this* moment. Belief is all well and good. But there must be skin on it—something we touch, see, hear, taste, and smell. In other words, it's the small daily stuff that does really matter.

So. Today, let us practice the sacrament of the blessed present.

Today, let us dance with manatees.

This is a book I've always wanted to write. I'm so glad the manatees made it possible.

* * * * *

"We should do this more often." A middle-aged man is speaking to a woman somewhat north of middle age standing at his side.

I am doing what I do best: Eavesdropping.

The couple is leaning on the upper deck railing of a Washington State Ferry on a summer day. We are headed across the Puget Sound, from Seattle toward the Kitsap Peninsula. I can tell it's their first ferry ride, first trip to the Pacific Northwest, and likely a very special occasion. The Olympic Mountains, still snow-tipped, fill our panorama. I have lived in this neck of the woods over thirty years, and this tranquil scene—a melding of pewter-blue water with a hunter-green tree line—has not yet failed to give me gooseflesh. Whenever I return from a trip, the mountains and water always reorient me. Listening and watching this couple, it is apparent that they too are plum-tickled, finding enchantment and solace in nature's pageant.

"We should do what?" she asks.

"Take these kind of trips," he tells her. He gestures, "Take the time to enjoy all of this. The fresh air, the mountains, the blue sky, for two weeks no kids or grandkids and nowhere to be and no time to be there. It's our chance to slow down."

"But we're doing it right now," the woman offers.

"Yes," the husband persists, "but think of all the opportunities and years we've missed." He begins the very long litany of all the trips that should have been, and each story gets more and more depressing.

I realize that I need to intervene. "Dude," I say, benevolently, "If you don't shut up, you'll miss this trip too."

"Wherever you are, be all there," Jim Elliot reminded us. Which is all well and good until we admit that we all practice a finely honed skill of expecting life to reside in an event or experience or occasion other than the one we are in right now.

There are those lucky moments when we recognize and embrace the here and now. And when that happens, I'll be if we don't want to bottle it up, and sell it on eBay. (This makes me think of the Transfiguration story in Mark's Gospel. Peter is so worked up he wants to build three

9

condos and call it permanent.) Or worse yet, we feel compelled to evaluate or measure each experience, as if a superlative is a requirement for its enjoyment. "That was the bestest," we update anyone who asks on our social media feed.

I was going to spend some time wrestling with the wisdom of Jim Elliot's statement, and distill it for a lecture, but Brian called me this morning with "an exciting opportunity." His name didn't ring a bell, but Brian chatted like he knew me well. And, it's not every day you get offered an exciting opportunity. Brian wanted me to have a free satellite dish. All for me. This kind of generosity makes you all tingly inside, doesn't it? I could get 500 channels, Brian told me. And all these options provide me "so much more to enjoy in life," Brian chirped (literally, he chirped). And (Brian's spiel had no pause button), I would never have to be "afraid of missing anything," because I could record all the good stuff. I didn't want to burden Brian with the fact that being faced with a lot of options—like standing in the grocery store trying to choose cereal or toothpaste—makes me want to beat my head against a metal pole, so 500 channels might send me straight to the floor in a fetal position. Instead, I tell Brian that while I was "in awe" of his offer to appreciate life, I asked if I could make my decision after I spend the day potting some new cuttings for my garden, filling my birdfeeders and taking a brief nap in my lawn chair. Brian was quiet. I'm not sure Brian understood.

While waiting for perfect, we pass on ordinary. While waiting for better, we don't give our best effort to good. While waiting for new and improved, we leach the joy right out of this, or any, moment.

There's nothing wrong with looking forward to something. Like my friend who likes to say, "I'm not going to have a midlife crisis until I can afford to buy a Mustang." Fair enough. But most of the time, Alfred E. Neuman is right: "Most of us don't know what we want in life, but we're sure that we haven't got it."

In the grocery store the other day I overheard another couple, discussing their list for a dinner party. "We need wine," he says. "We have that nice bottle of Cabernet at home," she tells him. "I'm not wasting a good bottle of wine on your mother," he huffs. This will be a dinner of goodwill and revelry, I think, and I'm sorry I'm going to miss it.

In a culture of lottery winners and bigger and louder and faster and newer and shinier, ordinary gets disoriented in the din. And savoring, well, that becomes a lost art.

Ordinary, like watching dusk settle while reading on the patio, counting nuthatches when they return to the feeder, enjoying a handful of fresh strawberries from the garden (they sit on the tongue with a sweetness that makes you believe in heaven) and playing golf with my son on the back lawn. Ordinary, yes. But a day without the heaviness of expectation, worry, or fear.

As I write this, I'm bemoaning one of the drawbacks of travel for work. Too often, when I return home, instead of seeing what is, I regret all that I have missed in my garden. Peonies no longer in full bloom, profligate and splendid. My favorite Japanese iris—with its short window of bloom—no longer exquisite, delicate, and arresting. And yet. There is Penelope, the first rose to bloom in my garden, but still bursting, each bloom the shade of soft pearl.

So, I do confess to whining about time flying by, or some other variation on jammed schedules, stretched resources, and altered expectations. But I've found the wisdom of May Sarton spot-on, and her sentiment is mine, "There is a slight lifting of the air so I can smell the earth for the first time, and yesterday I again took possession of my life here."

Tonight on Vashon, dusk gives the horizon more substance, the sky now the color of ink. And I think again about shadows, and I smile.

11

Shadows are those veins of disappointment, doubt, sorrow, disillusion, insecurity, disenchantment, un-fulfillment, heartache, or shame that can course through our psyche. I know that there will always be someone, usually in the name of God, to tell me that I need to pray more, or believe more, or try harder. (Not that any of this seems to help my blood pressure.)

However, I find comfort having someone say to me, "I don't know how you lost your way today, but if it's OK by you, I'll sit a spell with you on the back deck, just to see if we can't enjoy the colors the shadows make at dusk."

Yes. Even in the shadows, wherever you are, be all there.

● ● ● ● ●

A friend's son (in his thirties, from the big city) spent the weekend on Vashon Island. He asked his mother (my friend), "What are we going to do today?"

"What do you mean?" she asked.

"Are we going to sit around the house today and do nothing?"

I'm grinning real big as she tells me the story. Ahhh…wonderful, ordinary nothing. That'll sure get in the way of excitement.

Reminds me of another comment I overheard, "I want a different kind of life." I understand the sentiment; I just didn't know that life came in kinds. With the incessant pressure to live a life other than the one we have, we are susceptible to the same malady that plagued the guy at the ferry boat railing: missing out on the very life we long to live.

I have an idea. Can we eliminate the question, "What did you accomplish today?" Whenever anyone asks me, it makes my head spin, and I find myself scrambling for the right sentence just to impress the questioner.

I have a friend who jogs on the path next to Lake Washington, "for cardiovascular work," she insists. But she spends a good part of her walk stopped, standing there, just to look at the sky and the clouds. "It's OK," she says, "This is so much better for my heart."

How right she is.

Even in the unaccomplished ordinary, wherever you are, live with new eyes. Be here. Now.

This book is an invitation to practice, to savor the sacred present. And along the way, I hope this book is your invitation to dance with manatees. In case you are wondering, here's the fine print: This is not an advice book. This is not a motivational book. Which is not to say you won't find advice or motivation here. It's just that this is not an irresistible sales pitch, promising guaranteed treasures. "Lose weight in ten days." Or, "Learn to savor the moment in one afternoon, now!" Savoring life is not a test, or a contest, or a race, or a beauty pageant.

We will, however, heed Barry Lopez's wisdom: "The stories people tell have a way of taking care of them. If stories come to you, care for them. And learn to give them away where they are needed. Sometimes a person needs a story more than food to stay alive. That is why we put these stories in each other's memories. This is how people care for themselves."

So, we will tell lots of stories. And I invite you to enter the stories, and to allow the stories to enter you. Stories about…

> the gift of epiphanies willingness to be surprised, and to live glad hearted;
>
> the freedom to live from sufficiency and not scarcity;
>
> the permission to invest our whole heart, our whole self;
>
> to live unabashed and undaunted;
>
> to relish the gift of touch, and the spiritual grounding of the senses;
>
> the invitation to live undefended and without fear.

I'm glad we're on this journey together.

May Sarton used to say that she spent the first twenty minutes of every day wandering the garden (or wander your city block, or city park, or area near your home) looking for miracles. Try this ritual to start your day, no matter where you are. Or, spend twenty minutes just watching the way morning light bounces and reflects and illumines.

And if someone calls and asks what you are doing, say, "I'm watching for miracles. Do you want to join me?"

Chapter Two

We Are Wired to Be Present; We Are Wired to Dance

We are not human beings having a spiritual experience. We are spiritual beings having a human experience. —TEILHARD DE CHARDIN

Every child has known God,
Not the God of names,
Not the God of don'ts,
Not the God who ever does anything weird,
But the God who knows only four words.
And keeps repeating them, saying:
"Come Dance with Me, come dance."
—HAFIZ

After an event in Angel Fire, New Mexico, I drove in early morning light from Gardnerville, Nevada, through the Carson Valley to the Reno airport. The drive is framed by the Sierra Nevada Mountains, including the snow-laden peaks that cradle Lake Tahoe. There is no urgency and it is a quiet drive, miles of open, high-desert pastures, a canvas of camouflage, tan-speckled with congregations of cows. They are still, as if they were asked to pose for a photo. And inclined to please, they said yes.

Absorbing this medicine for hurry, or blue moods, I smile. I typically think of transit to airports (or waiting in airports) as time to fill or tolerate, on my way to what really matters.

I remember a statement made in *The Irish Times* by a Connemara man after he was arrested for a car accident. "There were plenty of onlookers, but no witnesses."

Hmmm. It's like the tourists who religiously follow the advice of travel journals, and miss the unanticipated "sacred places."

We've consumed many books or sermons about the correct way to live life. Which, sadly, we assume, is a life other than the one we have today. In other words, we haven't trusted that we are empowered to witness and savor *this* life.

On this morning drive, the tranquil backdrop gives my mind wandering room, which is always a good thing. A wandering mind makes space to absorb beauty and stillness with an affirmation of serenity.

I've needed to face the parts of my life that derail too easily. That's not fun to admit. I give way to exhaustion and resentment (they seem to go hand in hand, and I give myself grief for it). Have you ever had that…where you wake up one day—spirit drained—and wonder where the joy went, and why? It doesn't help that I've marinated in a world that is duty-bound to resolve or fix. No wonder we feel the weight of anything out of sync. I get a geyser of email, much of it uninvited. But I'm still seduced by many of the pitches, because they promise me a bigger and better life, one that makes a difference and breaks the bank every month. "What did you do of significance?" one asks, wondering if I make the kind of money I deserve to make. And I think, "Well, I don't know about the money, but I had a great chat with some cows in the Carson Valley this morning. And that did my heart good. Does that count?"

When it comes to significance, here's the deal: There is extravagant value in tending the soil of my soul.

• • • • •

In southern Michigan, I was raised in a religious tradition that used the word *grace*, but were too afraid to give in to it. Not unlike the faithful band of "believers" in the movie *Babette's Feast* who, when offered an extraordinarily generous gift of the feast-of-a-lifetime, make the decision to "taste" the wine, but not "enjoy it."

I was cajoled to believe in a God who was no different than an alcoholic father. This isn't hypothetical to me. Yes, I wanted his love, but was never sure which father would show up. So, I did my best to make him smile. And when he did smile, I would feel a shudder, wondering whether it was enough, or what I would do that would make his smile go away.

I know that scarcity affects how we see God. We have been weaned on the belief that our well-being is stuck in scarcity. Requiring us to earn our way out. It is no wonder that scarcity, not sufficiency, becomes our lens and our paradigm and our narrative. Scarcity affects how we see the world. Scarcity affects how we see the present moment.

I must be missing something.
This is too good to be true.
Can I trust this moment?
I know I don't deserve this.

If grace is dependent on God's mood or temperament or on my performance, the scales always tilt. And that never turns out well.

We do well to consider Rabbi Abraham Heschel's reminder, "We teach children how to measure and how to weigh. We fail to teach them how to revere, how to sense wonder and awe."

We savor, because this life, this day, this moment, is a gift.

And we sense wonder and awe because we are grounded in sufficiency.

I remember leading a retreat with an animated group of teachers — St. Augustine's in Vancouver, British Columbia. Their day of refueling before a new school year. Our topic, an invitation to create sanctuary, allowing us to honor habits that sustain our wellbeing.

We began the day going around a circle, each sharing memories from the summer. There were weddings and funerals and trips and reunions and adventures and celebrations in Parisian pubs after a World Cup victory.

"I have a heart condition," one young teacher began her turn. "And every year I get an MRI for assessment. Because I never know what the news will be, my temptation is caution and apprehension. Because of my condition, and afraid of the worst, I have always kept my physical activity to a minimum. Although I'll admit that the excuse does come in handy, 'I'd love to help out, but I have a heart condition.'"

We laughed.

"This year, after a clear MRI, my doctors told me that I needed more activity. Outdoors. Nothing strenuous. But still. Anyway, my summer was very different than normal. I biked and hiked and enjoyed the sky and water and the air. I loved being outdoors."

Well, I have a confession. I have lived most of my emotional and spiritual life with a heart condition. Because I have lived cautious and afraid, holding back my heart because of what it might cost, or require of me. Or fearing (running from) my brokenness, not believing that an open and broken heart is an invitation to live my days giving, creating, embracing, connecting, savoring, and celebrating. It is no wonder that, too often, I do not see.

Hundreds of years ago, in an era much more fraught than ours, St. Francis learned to live without holding back his heart. His antidote to confusion and paralysis was a return to simplicity, one step at a time, one person at a time, one good thing at a time, the right-in-front-of-you idea of searching for the light even while living with the darkness. His genius was that he saw what was hidden in plain sight. It was so simple it is almost impossible to see; we are wired to be present.

• • • • •

On NPR's *This American Life*, Ira Glass interviewed a young woman, a singer with a Riverdance troupe. She told how one day, the troupe collectively decided to purchase a batch of lottery tickets. The plan (buoyed by sheer conviction and blind faith) seemed simple enough. Such a large purchase would increase their odds of winning, and with the considerable prize money, they could share the proceeds.

After winning (a foregone conclusion in their minds), they had determined they would quit Riverdance, and use the money to do whatever it was they really wanted to do: go back to school, buy a house, seek a new vocation, and so on. Behind each of their wishes, you could read the longing for a change, for a new direction in their lives.

On the evening the lottery winner was to be announced, the troupe danced their "final" performance. The singer described how a kind of ecstasy swept up the entire troupe, as they danced and sang wholehearted and unabashed. In their hearts, all the performers knew this would be their winning night, the night they would be released from the monotony of their lives. All of them knew as well, as they danced and sang, that they were giving, creating, living, and celebrating their best performance ever. Afterward, the audience, understandably, went wild. Something truly amazing had taken place.

The drawing was held. Not one troupe ticket held the winning number. They did not win the lottery. To a person, they couldn't believe that their intention—or confidence—had failed them.

And yet.[1]

Look at what happened. Their performance provided a container—a liturgy or sacred space—for some awakening of that which lay dormant in their souls. In fact, the troupe, literally, transcended the dance itself.

They were engaged. They were totally alive and present. And, as it turns out, they did receive what they wished for. In other words, once the troupe gave up the need to force a great performance, they simply danced with an open heart.

During our Vancouver teachers' retreat, we made a list of all the gifts born in the sacrament of the present: vulnerability, empathy, inclusion, compassion, presence, authenticity, the permission to be grounded…. Looking at the list, I made the observation that while we hunger for these gifts, it will take a toll, because every one of them invites us to live with and from our whole heart.

If only we have eyes to see.

Or, perhaps (I will tell myself), if only we can surrender expectations that, in the end, prevent us from seeing. Such as anticipated lottery winnings, I suppose…with the promise that life can be found "if only" or "when." Or in my case, having succumbed to some unnamed fear that keeps me from living an "unabashed life." ("What would they think?")

Our knee-jerk reaction, of course, is to figure it all out, some sort of checklist for "living fully present." (There's the rub. Apparently, it's not authenticity or intimacy I want. It's certainty and security that I'm after.)

There is something essential for us to grasp here. Regardless of our intent (or desire, or wish, or prayer), "if only we had eyes to see" is not about trying harder or learning a new skill set. Instead, just as the dance troupe learned, we recognize that freedom happens only when we can let go.

"Once you have grace," wrote Thomas Merton, "you are free. Without it, you cannot help doing the things you know you should not do, and that you know you don't really want to do."

Yes. And Amen. Because here's the deal: Living from an open heart always takes us beyond our ego. We do not need to live defensive. And what spills from an open heart? An invitation to live generous, benevolent, grateful, compassionate, and kind…to savor the sacrament of the present moment.

In an episode of *The West Wing*, C.J. Cregg (White House chief of staff) is wired, tense and distracted. Her love interest shows up, middle of the workday, at her White House office, "to take her for a walk." She consents (but not without a fight, you know, so much "to do"). On the walk, she fidgets and asks, "So, what was so important, taking this walk?"

He says, "Just to see."

"Well," she tells him, "this is not the day for it."

It made me laugh out loud. Sure, I want to live this moment mindful of the sacred, but this is not the day for it. As if there is a special day for it?

In our Western mindset, living in the present becomes a staged event. Staged to be "spiritual." As if this is something we must orchestrate. Or arrange. And we sit stewing in the juices of our self-consciousness: "Am I present? What am I doing right or wrong?" All the while, missing the point.

We don't need the Sierra Nevadas (or any breathtaking vista for that matter) to have moments that invite us to stop, pay attention, and be at home in our own skin.

Thomas Merton said, "One of the best things for me when I went to the hermitage was being attentive to the times of the day: when the birds began to sing, and the deer came out of the morning fog, and the sun came up—while in the monastery, summer or winter, Lauds is at the same hour. The reason why we don't take time is a feeling that we have to keep moving. This is a real sickness. Today time is commodity, and for each one of us time is mortgaged. We experience time as unlimited indebtedness. We are sharecroppers of time. We are threatened by a chain reaction: overwork-overstimulation-overcompensation-overkill."

As my southern grandmother would say, "That'll preach." As long as we live in oblivion, distracted or waiting, we bury the very things that might set us free. Yes, I love this paradigm; to be set free is to live from our DNA.

A Hasidic rabbi was interrupted by one of his followers while he was tending his garden, "What would you do, rabbi," the student asked, "if you knew the messiah was coming today?" Stroking his beard and pursing his lips, the rabbi replied, "Well, I would continue to water my garden."

So, before we decipher life, let us see life.

Before we wish for another life, let us feel this life.

Before we give in to "if only," let us listen to this moment.

Before we succumb to "someday," let us inhale this day.

Before we trade in this life for the life we "should" have, let us taste this life.

Each of the above is a choice; a choice to be open. To be available. To be curious. To be alive. To be willing to be surprised by joy. To know there is power in the word *enough*.

Similar to St. Thérèse, St. Francis always preserved childhood wonder. He lived Matthew's Gospel message, "Unless you turn and become like children, you will never enter the kingdom of heaven. Whoever humbles himself like this child, he is the greatest in the kingdom of heaven."

Jesus reinforcing the message, "I praise you, Father, Lord of heaven and earth, because you have hidden these things from the wise and learned, and revealed them to little children" (Matthew 11:25).

It reminds me of Henry Miller's quote, "The aim of life is to live, and to live means to be aware, joyously, drunkenly, serenely. We live at the edge of the miraculous." In other words, to make space for what is dormant in our soul. We are wired with the capacity to honor the present, in every encounter and relationship. In fact, you're doing that now, as you read and reflect.

We are wired to honor the dignity that is reflected by God's goodness and grace.

This means, as Simone Weil reminds us in *Gravity and Grace*, "In everything which gives us the pure authentic feeling of beauty there really is the presence of God. There is as it were an incarnation of God in the world and it is indicated by beauty. The beautiful is the experimental proof that the incarnation is possible."[2]

"Count me in," I say. "What's the next step?"

But then patience has never been my strong suit.

The Navajo Indians would tell me to go for a walk. It doesn't have to be a long walk. And to say this prayer as I go...

> In beauty may I walk
> All day long may I walk
> Through returning seasons may I walk
> On the trail marked with pollen may I walk
> With grasshoppers about my feet may I walk
> With dew about my feet may I walk
> With beauty may I walk
> With beauty behind me may I walk
> With beauty above me may I walk
> With beauty below me may I walk
> With beauty all around me may I walk
> In old age wandering on a trail of beauty, lively may I walk
> In old age wandering on a trail of beauty, living may I walk
> It is finished in beauty
> It is finished in beauty

Walking or not, I try my best to follow Mary Oliver's instructions for life: "Pay attention. Be astonished. Tell about it."

I can assure you that when you practice Mary's instructions, "what's next" will take care of itself.

Try This

Change your greeting…from "What did you do (whether this day or this week)?" to "Tell me about your last duckling moment."

If you talk with anyone today, start with a question distinctive from "What did you do?" You know, like "What made you giggle?" or "What's your favorite dessert?" or "Do red poppies make you smile?"

Chapter Three

Savoring Is the Portal; Gratitude Is the Fuel

Dear God, I didn't think orange went with purple, until I saw the last sunset You made on Tuesday. That was cool. — SARA, *Children's Letters to God*

Instead of trying to name it, I just stand there and try to savor it, to figure out how to hold that peace in my heart and how to take it with me, if I can. — RICK BASS

Gratitude dances through the open windows of our hearts. We cannot force it. We cannot create it. And we can certainly close our windows to keep it out. But we can also keep them open and be ready for the joy when it comes. — LEW SMEDES

I live on an island. There is no bridge. The only way on or off the island is a ferry. It's our way of life here. If you're in a hurry, island life is not for you. Whenever I return home from any speaking trip, I land late at night, and navigate my car from the airport to the ferry terminal, hoping that the schedule works in my favor. Travel can do a number on you, with outbreaks of stress and strain. I'm always eager to be home. When I crest the hill in West Seattle, I can see Vashon Island and the ferry terminal, and the lights of the ferry crossing the Puget Sound. And my heartbeat slows. And it hits me; the ferry is my portal to home.

Two things happen in any portal. A place to enter into, and a place to leave something behind.

Savoring is the portal to the sacrament of the present.

Like most small towns in America, summer brings a festival. (Even when several weeks from summer, it never hurts to anticipate.) On Vashon Island, we celebrate the Strawberry Festival. A weekend of festivity, gastronomic adventure and community identity. A long time ago, there were strawberry fields on our island. No more. Even so, the festival name persists. (I think in large part because those enormous banners are very expensive to replace.)

On festival weekend, Saturday night is dance night. We're a one-horse, one-street town. So, our main street is shut down, and becomes our dance floor under dusk light that lingers until well past ten.

At 7 p.m., the Portage Fill-Harmonic fills the night air with big band swing music. The musicians are all islanders who play for the love of music. We know them as our neighbors, carrying out their daily jobs, but on this night, it is their avocation, which takes center stage. The cares of the world drift into the sky on the wings of the music.

At 9 p.m., we shift gears, and the mood gives way to Great Divide and old-time Rock and Roll (for the uninitiated, this is music which predates 1973). And everybody dances.

My son, Zach—then, aged ten—stirred by the music, charged to the front of the pack, near the stage. And he began to…well, I'm not sure what to call what he began to do. It was a combination of jiujitsu and tai chi and *Saturday Night Fever*. All fueled by sheer and unabashed delight.

Other dancers began to make room for this enthusiastic young artiste. And his presence was apparent. People near me—as I stood near the back of the crowd—began to point and laugh, out of solidarity

I suppose, but even so, I could feel my heart skip a beat.

"Look at that kid," they said. (Actually, since this is a small island, they said, "Look at Terry's kid.")

I took a step forward. I confess to you that my knee-jerk response was to go toward the stage, in order to rescue or protect my son. Rescue from what, I wonder? From fear or embarrassment or awkwardness or shame? Is public opinion that severe? "What will they think?" swirls, a question still ingrained from my childhood. Did I fear that others would consider his spectacle extravagant and unrestrained? (Lord knows I'd hate to have a group uncomfortable on my account, just because I was delighted.)

We all wrestle with some internal governor prescribing some need for moderation or temperance, which translates, "It's time to put the kibosh on all manner of joy or ecstasy or elation or, God forbid, wholeheartedness." Here's the deal: When we give way to any such shackling measure, we put a lid on our passion and our spirit, and we short-circuit the bounty and generosity that would spill from our heart.

This all begs the question: What is the reason we internalize this script, and how does it procure its power? In other words…why, oh why, do we allow ourselves to live so small?

I am glad, on that Saturday night, I did not take a second step.

Instead, I took a step back.

Because I realized that what I felt was not shame. It was not chagrin. No. What I felt, was pride. My son experiencing and touching and relishing what I too desired. I recognized that there will be many experiences in his life that will dampen or quench that spirit, and I don't want to be one of them. Through my tears, I watched him dance.

After two songs he raced back to us, animated, "Mom and Dad, did you see that? Wasn't I great?"

"Yes, indeed, son. You were great."

At some point every single one of us is connected to a life source, or life force—a grounded place of ecstasy, joy, and hope.

We are wired. And it wells up and spills out to all around us.

My son teaches me that savoring is the portal to the present moment.

There are no manatees on Vashon. But there was dancing nonetheless, and the joy resonated and reverberated.

• • • • •

Before we get ahead of ourselves, let us pause and remember that savoring isn't something you add or acquire. Unabashed joy is already inside. It springs from within. It is a well of abundance that you draw from.

So, savoring is not a technique. And savoring is never an end unto itself. It is always fueled by gratitude. And gratitude lights up our senses. We enter into, we show up to the needs and cares of *this* day. I suppose that it's a chicken or egg scenario. And which comes first, I'm not sure.

I do know that savoring makes space for gratitude. And gratitude begets savoring. Either way, we find ourselves smack dab in the middle of the present.

It is coffee hour on a summer Sunday—that time after church service when we sip coffee (or if we're brave, some unidentifiable fruit juice) and chat about the weather, the week's news, or if it's memorable, the sermon. Whatever we're talking about, there are times when we're aware of a self-conscious nudge to keep up appearances; this is, after all, church.

The laughter of children drifts in from outside. One boy, maybe five years old, runs into the fellowship hall looking for his mother—his face flushed, his hair supercharged, his pants grass-stained. His mother hides her irritation with skill, but not without effort, "What in God's name happened to you?"

"Mom, I just needed to tell you that I made a new friend," the boy reports, and he bolts back out the door. Sympathetic onlookers shake their heads, many thankful that their days of dealing with such shenanigans are over. They return to their conversation. Most didn't notice that one of their own, he long past seventy, snuck out the back door to join the game of hide-and-seek on the church lawn.

It's been a demarcation week in the Pacific Northwest...the sky opened up and rain drummed the rooftop and windows, early warning for our first winterish storm, wind gusts up to forty mph. Trees down, branches splintered, and hemlock needles litter the roadways, giving the appearance of a caramel-colored sisal carpet. Small boughs of fir are haphazardly scattered about. I'm driving for a 5:00 a.m. ferry, and a flight headed to the East Coast. I tell myself that garden cleanup can wait. And that somehow this untidiness may have been intended to feed my soul. A landscape unabashed, unencumbered and, best of all, unafraid of imperfection. Now tonight, 2,800 miles away, my host is navigating the meandering roadways near the Shenandoah National Park (Virginia). Tomorrow I will lead a retreat with a group from three Episcopal dioceses. At the retreat center, I step out of the car and the night sky is a kaleidoscope of stars on a coal-black canvas, save for the smudge of the Milky Way and a sliver of a moon, as if heaven's door were left ajar.

My garden, the Shenandoah sky, and the five-year-old boy in the fellowship hall are all kindred souls of sorts. They have each tapped into something. Carl Jung called it numinosity. Jean-Pierre de Caussade called it the sacrament of the present.

I like to call it petite miracle wandering. (Try that out when someone asks, "What did you do today?" "Well, I spent some time petite miracle wandering.")

Numinosity is the potential for unexpected mystery and insight where one comes into the unshakable presence of the divine; a sacred transformative space that integrates and heals the mind, body, soul, and spirit. Bottom line: where one feels fully and totally alive. When I danced with manatees, I didn't know there was a word for it. I do now. And I know that numinosity is essential.

How do I "acquire" it? Well...that is the question.

This past week, I actually overheard someone say, "Finally, this is what I've been waiting for." I don't remember what the THIS was, but, even so. I know what he meant. I have the same kind of list.

But let's not get our shorts in a knot chasing regret. Every one of us knows the sadness that comes with missing the moment. Every one of us has kept parts of our soul in check. And yes, we all have days that are not in the script (you know, days that feel like the complete absence of numinosity or anything divine).

Like this past week. I was out of sorts, so I spent afternoons yanking weeds, fighting with the people I love, and frustrated with my work. I lived petty. And to top it off, I gave myself a good deal of grief about it, thinking I was above all of that. But then, that's where we get off track. We think that spiritual experience—the sacred present—is like a stock portfolio. Something we accumulate and measure.

But here's the deal: The sacrament of the present (numinosity), begins with acceptance. With savoring. Savoring *this* day. Savoring *this* self. This imperfect, fractured, flawed, sometimes torn-to-pieces self.

I agree with Thomas Moore. "I'd rather be a dysfunctional soul than a well-adjusted robot."

As to how I acquire it, maybe I should take Indiana Jones's lead. Remember *Raiders of the Lost Ark*?

Indiana Jones: "Get back to Cairo, get us some transport to England. Boat, plane, anything...Meet me at Omar's. Be ready for me; I'm going after that truck."

Sallah: "How?"

Indiana Jones: "I don't know. I'm making this up as I go."

OK, if push comes to shove, I do have a couple suggestions.

One. Let the music of daily life be a salve. The music chatter from the birds at the feeder, the babble of the brook, the breeze through the trees, the children playing on the patio, the splash from the fountain, Bruce Springsteen singing "This little light of mine," on the stereo.

In the quirky movie *Joe Versus the Volcano*, Tom Hanks's character tells a mariachi band, "Play us a song what would drive us insane, that would make our hearts swell and burst." It reminded me of Kerouac's little bar in Mexico (from *On the Road*). He says that was the only time he ever got to hear music played loud enough.

Yes, the music of the ordinary. I can't say it better than Kent Nerburn in his book *Small Graces*:

Do we really need much more than this?

To honor the dawn.

To visit a garden.

To talk to a friend.

To contemplate a cloud.

To cherish a meal.

To bow our heads before the mystery of the day.

Are these not enough?

Two. Take a piece of paper and write. Write from the heart of a five-year-old standing grass-stained in the church fellowship hall, beaming at his mama. Tell me what you love.

You know, what takes you, even momentarily out of an overtly conscious view of the world (away from public opinion, or what is correct, or what is deemed appropriate)?

Tell me about your petite miracle wandering. What transports you, unburdens you, allows you to wallow in the expansive reach of grace, letting it wash over you, suspending explanation and justification? (I can tell you that when life begins to squeeze me, I can count on the smell from a skillet with garlic in butter, a vase with a fresh-cut rose, and Mozart wafting through the house.)

It is not easy is it, this catch-22 of literally being in the moment, suspended by joy, without the safety net of cerebral clarity?

When the young boy walks back into the fellowship hall, he's now holding the hand of the older man. Both are flushed in the cheeks. They've come in for another cookie. You hear comments whispered by others in the room.

"What's he thinking? He's going to have another heart attack if he's not careful!"

"That poor mother. That boy is a handful."

"I wish those kids wouldn't come in here with those dirty shoes."

One of the women serving coffee asks the older man, "We'll see you tomorrow night? Can I ask you a question about the agenda for our committee meeting?"

"Not now," he says, "First, I've got to tell you about this frog we found behind the back of the church."

Try this. If someone asks you what you did today (don't worry, someone will ask), say, "I made a new friend, and found a frog. Can I tell you about it?"

In the church fellowship hall after frog hunting, the young boy and his new friend the old man become for one another witnesses…a reminder that the sacrament of the present moment is available to all, with no exceptions. And in that sacrament, we invite and welcome and care and heal. This sacrament is not confined, it spills. And the good news is that you never know to what extent.

This we know for certain. When we live in the present, it spills. Savoring spills. Gratitude spills. Put simply; we are witnesses for one another.

That's why I keep the
gates of my heart open
'cause you never know
where love might be
I leave a crack in my defenses
and let the unexpected carry me
—LARRY MURANTE

On March 3, 2013, I walked the Edmund Pettus Bridge in Selma (Alabama) to commemorate Bloody Sunday. To commemorate courageous and spirited individuals who were willing to say that this life-force of joy and hope and justice and reconciliation is available to all. These marchers were told, "Not now. Don't rock the boat now." Public opinion rears its ugly head again...and thankfully those who marched or sang or danced or sat, did not listen: John Lewis, Ralph Abernathy, Martin Luther King, Jr., and Sister Mary Antona Ebo of the Franciscan Sisters of Mary — the first black nun to march.

At a recent concert with Vashon's local Free Range Folk Choir, we savored music from around the world, including music from South Africa. The story is told about the tactics police would use to dissuade any "protest" gatherings during apartheid. What the police couldn't stop was church, where South Africans worshiped and sang. And at some point, during church, the members would stand, singing, and walk out of the church. When confronted by the police, they responded, "But we're not protesting, we're singing."

I witnessed the sacrament of the present moment as a life force for good, for celebration, for meaning, for compassion, for justice...alive and well in Selma, on a bridge.

I witnessed the sacrament of the present in the singing of South African worshippers...

And I witnessed the sacrament of the present moment here on Vashon Island, beholding my ten-year-old son dance his heart out. When we don't play small...

We honor the heart.

We savor miracles in ordinary moments.

We let joy ring out.

We nurture hope.

We right wrongs.

We let freedom ring.

We let dancers dance.

We let hope live.

One younger friend told me about a life crossroads, which felt weighted by conundrum. I asked, "So what's next?"

She replied, "I'm just waiting for God to show me what he wants from me."

"OK," I said to her. "But in the meantime, you know, until you have your life and self figured out and straightened out, I have a suggestion: Live this day, with this self, without holding back. Today; savor, doubt, embrace, question, wrestle, give, risk, love, fall down, get up, accept your incomplete and fractured self, know that anything worth doing is worth doing badly, speak from your whole heart, and whenever you can, lavish excessive compassion and mercy and healing and hope and second chances and grace and restoration and kindness on anyone who crosses your path. Who knows, we may love one another into existence. And I'm sure God won't mind."

Try This

Find a place to sit or a place to walk. Practice going to that spot at least once a day just to stop, to quit, to let your soul catch up. Think about this: What does it mean for our soul to "catch up"?

Chapter Four

We Are Present—Obstacles, Messiness, and All

Recovering the sacred is remembering something we've forgotten, something we may have hidden from ourselves. It is about uncovering and discovering the innate wholeness in ourselves and in the world.—Dr. Naomi Rachel Remen

[When I am not grounded] I believe that whatever I seek in miracles, the sacred, intervention of the divine is not in a place where I am now—in a place other than this moment. They have this in common: we don't look at the world around us as places where God lives.—Rabbi Abraham Heschel

In the HBO documentary *Last Letters Home*, Paula Zasadny, mother of nineteen-year-old Specialist Holly McGeogh (killed by a bomb in Kirkuk), talks about a visit from officers in dress uniform.

"It was the lightest tap on my door that I've ever heard in my life," says Zasadny. "I opened the door and I see the men in the dress greens and I knew. I immediately knew. But I thought that if, as long as I didn't let him in, he couldn't tell me. Then it—none of that would've happened. So, he kept saying, "'Ma'am; I need to come in.' And I kept telling him, 'I'm sorry, but you can't come in.'"[3]

I cannot relate to Paula Zasadny's loss.

But I can relate to "light taps at the door," whether real or imagined. So can you. We all have parts of our life that unravel or splinter or deaden or reduce us to thunderstruck. While we never know what the trigger (whether immense or trivial) may be, while we never know whether it will be wrapped in tragedy or hurt or misunderstanding or simply accumulated aggravation, we do know that it will be, somehow, woven into the fabric or our days.

> "Real isn't how you are made," said the Skin Horse (the beloved rocking horse in *The Velveteen Rabbit*). "It's a thing that happens to you. When a child loves you for a long, long time, not just to play with, but REALLY loves you, then you become Real."
>
> "Does it hurt?" asked the Rabbit.
>
> "Sometimes," said the Skin Horse, for he was always truthful. "When you are Real you don't mind being hurt."

Chapters two and three are all well and good. We are wired to be present. And savoring is the portal to the present. However, life turns left. So, let's not pretend otherwise. Dancing with manatees is easy to say. And easy to read. And it is most certainly an invitation to the sacrament of the present moment. But saying and doing are two different things.

I know this: Some days I do "mind" being unraveled. And being hurt. And I want to run away. Or I want someone to fix it. Or I want to tell whoever or whatever is tapping at my door, "You can't come in."

"OK Terry, I'm tracking with you, that this life is about being present (mindful and attentive). But help me with the part of my mind and spirit that needs the sacrament of the present moment to be choreographed. Or, at the very least, free from muddle."

In our last chapter, we talked about portals creating space in our hearts to receive gifts of grace. The good news is that this grace is alive and well, even when encumbered by the messiness of daily life. It recalls Marcel Proust's observation that "the real voyage of discovery consists not in seeking new landscapes, but in having new eyes." St. Francis was even more specific, seeing God in both the dirt and the worms, seeing God in both the splendor and the misery.

The movie *Crimes of the Heart* (based on the Pulitzer Prize–winning play written by Beth Henley) is the story about three sisters surviving crisis after crisis in a small Mississippi town. The youngest, Rebecca (or "Babe"), finds a sort of solace in an almost comical practice, contorting her body in order to stick her head into the oven. One day, older sister Meg asks, exasperated, "Why'd you do it, Babe? Why'd you put your head in the oven?"

Babe: "I don't know...I'm having a bad day."

Meg: "Well...we've got to find a way to get you through these bad days."

If we're honest, we know that there are days when we feel certain that we just can't get through.

I remember an exchange in 2014 after the news about Robin Williams. I didn't expect it to hit me so viscerally. But it did. "That can't be," I kept saying out loud, to no one in particular. It's not easy because we see people who make us laugh and bring us joy, and hope that humor is a safeguard, or at the least makes us less susceptible, even to the illness of depression. Reading the opinion pieces about suicide, I realized that the news was visceral because we all know there are tipping points; we just don't always know when or where or why. And for whatever reason, we don't believe that mercy is our benediction.

My favorite scene in the movie *Forrest Gump* is one where Jenny (Forrest's girlfriend for life) stands in front of a dilapidated house. The house represents years of abuse and disappointment from her childhood. As she faces the demons of her past, she begins to pick up rocks and hurl them—with every scrap of her being—toward the house. She is, possibly for the first time, acknowledging years of anger, pain, hatred, and fear. She eventually collapses to the ground and Forrest Gump's simple commentary is this: "Sometimes there just aren't enough rocks."

We don't enjoy, let alone pray for, untidiness. Our craving is understandable: to fix and repair and tidy and give advice. And we find comfort bringing God into the collusion. So, we pray to a God that has a plan, and a way to solve. And I always wonder what this false certainty takes care of. And ask, why are we so afraid of mystery?

On the ferry this week, I am eavesdropping, honoring one of my cardinal rules: Eavesdropping on a good conversation always eclipses whatever else may be on my list. Two women are commiserating about life's vicissitudes. They tell stories filled with culprits and villains. I'll give you the abridged version…

There are parents not talking with grown children. There are life-threatening medical conditions. There are relationships gone awry. There are friends who turn out to be not real friends. There are betrayals and secrets. And there are men who are idiots. (I could have guessed that last one.)

We all have our sad places. No matter how we "clean up," we all have our cracks in the façade.

As if that's not bad enough, we live in a world that expects us to apologize for any weakness or sorrow. "I'm sorry," the young woman says, as she tells me about a very challenging time in her life, wiping away her tears. "I shouldn't feel this way."

Excuse me? "I'm sorry." Sorry for being which…Normal? Or sad? Or real?

(Just a reminder: anytime the word *should*—or *shouldn't*—is added to any sentence, things turn sour in a real hurry.)

"Life is difficult," Scott Peck wrote in *The Road Less Traveled*. Yes. And sometimes it feels like it takes us to the breaking point. So, if sticking our head in the oven is not the answer, what can we do?

In 1914, famed explorer Sir Ernest Shackleton set out from England on an expedition to cross the continent of Antarctica. He posted this brief notice: "Men wanted for hazardous journey. Small wages. Bitter cold. Long months of complete darkness. Constant danger. Safe return doubtful. Honour and recognition in case of success."

Five thousand men applied. Twenty-eight men began the voyage. The expedition did not (to put it mildly) go as planned. What transpired is breathtaking and, quite literally, beyond belief. The crew spent 635 days, surviving cold, their ship crushed by ice, months of darkness, and living in makeshift camps in cramped quarters.

I recommend watching the documentary *The Endurance*, which features actual footage taken by expedition member Frank Hurley and includes interviews with surviving relatives, plus archived audio interviews with expedition members. One day away from their destination, Vahsel Bay (in the Antarctic Circle), surrounded by an unforeseen heavy ice flow, the *Endurance* halted. Stuck, the crew spent the winter months living on a stranded ship. After months, Shackleton made the decision to abandon ship and continue on foot (which proved fortuitous as they watched the *Endurance* crushed by the ice and claimed by the sea).

In lifeboats, the crew found its way to Elephant Island, with hope fleeting. Against all odds, Shackleton and five crew members boarded one small lifeboat (leaving the others for future rescue), spending three weeks crossing eight hundred miles of frigid, raging ocean.

After reaching South Georgia Island (ironically, where their expedition had begun over a year previous), the starved and frostbitten men found themselves on the wrong side of the island, which meant that they needed to cross a severe mountainous terrain, a journey never attempted or completed before.

Facing almost certain death that morning, Shackleton wrote in his journal: "We passed through the narrow mouth of the cove with the ugly rocks and waving kelp close on either side, turned to the east, and sailed merrily up the bay as the sun broke through the mists and made the tossing waves sparkle around us. We were a curious-looking party on that bright morning, but we were feeling happy. We even broke into song, and, but for our Robinson Crusoe appearance, a casual observer might have taken us for a picnic party sailing in a Norwegian fjord or one of the beautiful sounds of the west coast of New Zealand."

He said "happy"? Yes, he did. And he found the sacrament of the present, even when all options appeared gone.

I find incredible inspiration—and hope—in such stories.

Here's another, about the tragic bombing in the town of Omagh, Northern Ireland. In 1998, twenty-nine people died as a result of the attack and approximately 220 people were injured; the attack was described by the BBC as "Northern Ireland's worst single terrorist atrocity" and by British Prime Minister Tony Blair as an "appalling act of savagery and evil."

After the attack, Daryl Simpson created the Omagh Community Youth Choir of Catholic and Protestant teenagers, to use music as a way to begin the healing. Give yourself a treat and watch them on YouTube singing U2's "Love Rescue Me."

So, yes, messiness, disappointment, misfortune and heartbreak can be a part of my life. However, they are not the whole of my life. These young people from Ireland understand that. Their source of healing? Not advice. Not shoulds. Not sermons. They let the pain and messiness come in, and in that place, they embrace the sacrament of the present moment. How do they do that? They encircle and swathe the pain with song.

Some time back I was invited to lecture on intimacy (which is brave, considering that more often than not, I haven't a clue). When

I was writing my lecture, I asked my eight-year-old son, Zach, what to say. He said, "Dad, tell them that hugs and kisses wouldn't hurt." Thank you son. End of lecture.

Today, my music—my healing place—is my garden. I've been home almost one month. A gift. It's my first non-travel month in many years. I sit on the patio every night at dusk, listening to the sound of water cascading into the pond. The English roses nearby have begun their second pageant, not as outrageous as the first, but with a soft beauty that melts the heart. And the music of Keb' Mo' fills the air. It reminds me that sanctuary is a dose of grace. Because gifts (stillness, calm, mystery) are bestowed. Which means we can't orchestrate them. But we can make space. And in that space, blessedly receive.

● ● ● ● ●

I woke up on the floor of the hotel foyer. I saw a lot of blood. I didn't remember falling. Let's just say that my week didn't go quite as planned. Brandie and Della had dropped me off, after a speaking event in Spokane, Washington, where I talked with the Inland Empire Garden Club about how gardening is good for the spirit. Brandie had asked Della to wait before they left the curb. Because of that, she saw me when I fell.

I said, "I'll be OK," holding paper towels over my eye and nose.

"No," she said, "you're going to the hospital."

No reason to argue with a woman, especially when she's right. They took me to the ER. And stayed until I was discharged. I learned that while coughing deeply, I passed out, and face-planted. The floor won. Who knew? There's a first for everything.

I'm not a fan of moral lessons for every episode. "Everything happens for a reason," I heard one preacher say. Well, maybe. But that's only if you need everything to be tidy. I'm not sure that life is about tidiness. Maybe life happens when it's not tidy. When it doesn't make sense. When there's blood on the floor. Paying attention to the life that is, and not just the lessons to be learned. If I'm impatient to find the lesson, I miss every opportunity to stop and just see. To not rush by. Who knows, maybe to create a window where I'm open and available to receive.

In a memorable M*A*S*H* episode, there is a wounded bombardier who thinks he is Jesus. The camp is mixed. Some say he's crazy, but most say he's "acting" in order to get discharged from the army. One person in camp believes him: Radar O'Reilly. It's time for the man's release. Radar walks out to the jeep where the man sits. "Excuse me, Jesus, sir. Could you bless my friend?"

"Yes," the man replies.

And Radar pulls his teddy bear from behind his back. Jesus blesses the bear.

"Excuse me, Jesus, sir. Could you bless me?"

"Yes, Radar."

Radar steps back in deference. "Thank you. And my name. It's not Radar, sir. It's Walter."

Bless me.

Let's pause here. We embrace the sacrament of the present moment precisely because we are not encumbered by anxiety or disquiet or the need to impress. In other words, our spirit is safe. What is Radar asking for? Many say that to "be blessed" is to be granted God's favor and protection. To be safe even in the darkest time. (And just for the record, this is not a game rigged in the favor of people with more faith or favor. Blessing never plays favorites.) Other definitions of blessing include bringing welcome pleasure or relief. And another, to be consecrated or made holy.

Regardless of the definition, there is good news in all of this. We live in a world where we are bombarded—daily—by the need to achieve, or pursue; where we are rewarded by consuming and having more, or by being "somebody." So, we create layers between what is and what should be. And we feel less at home. (Even if that achieving is a semblance of togetherness. You know, like, no embarrassing blood on the face.)

To be blessed, is to know that place of no striving.

To be blessed, is to know that place of rest and dignity.

To be blessed, is to know that I am loved by a gracious Creator, and that I can own and celebrate my identity—this identity—knowing that it, and it alone, is enough.

I sit in the ER. Noise hums from monitoring machines. The crackle over the radio, an ambulance calling in, reading the vital signs. Conversations between ER staff, "What are you doing for vacation?" "Nothing."

I like taking it all in with a new appreciation after reading Victoria Sweet's book *God's Hotel,* drawing from the life and medicine of Hildegard of Bingen, and the power of little things on the journey toward healing. I chat with the doc while she stitches up my eyebrow.

"What do you do?" she asks.

"Find ways to help keep people sane in a hurried and distracted world," I tell her.

"Oh, you should come talk to our staff."

"That would be great," I say. "I'd be glad to do it in exchange for the ER invoice." (Yes, I'm sure she smiled.)

While I'm passing the time (waiting for the CT scan), I feel equal parts stupid, lucky (no broken bones in my face), inconvenienced, curious, resigned, and listening to my ADHD self tell me, "It's time to get up and go. You've got stuff to do."

We need a regular reminder: vulnerability is not a bad crossroads. We do need to look out for the permission and freedom to receive, to remember that this isn't a solo endeavor. We do need one another. To bless and be blessed. To care and be cared for. To invite and be invited to dance.

Messiness exposes vulnerability. I will admit, vulnerability is not my strong suit. I do prefer self-sufficiency. And rising above. And yet, self-reliance sounds laudable, but can be an obstacle, because it is difficult to say the words "help" or "thank you." So, here's the good news: There is power in embracing vulnerability. And vulnerability never exempts us from the sacrament of the present. Because vulnerability allows us to rest in that touch, that blessing.

The hospital cleared me to take my early morning flight. I am grateful, but rushing past anything where life is real, is not always a good idea. We all know what it's like to not be seen. Or to be missed. Or misunderstood. Or marginalized. To not be real. (And we tend to exaggerate it all by internalizing the tapes, playing them, Lord knows why, in the end buying whatever rhetoric and fabrication they are selling.)

This much is certain: If I need my life to be uncluttered, I'm not available to receive a blessing.

The day after my face-plant, I was with the good people at University United Methodist Church in Syracuse, New York, for Lent. Their theme, "Let Justice Roll Down." And my sermon title, "Jesus in Skin."

Before church, there is a breakfast in the basement. Eggs, sausage, pancakes, gravy, the works. The kind a southern grandmother would cook for her grandson. It's free to the community. The room is filled with people. Folks from the neighborhood. Some from the street. Some homeless, or under the weight of poverty. A few parishioners and volunteers. So yes. Eccentrics. Loners. Characters. (My swollen face and black eye did not look out of place. My suit, however, did.)

It would not be unkind to say that the collection of people at breakfast represented groups we tend to exclude from our churches. We like things tidy, don't we? But then, that's the best part about grace and mercy and embracing the sacrament of the present moment... Tidiness is not required.

I confess that I have spent much of my life making sure that I've earned enough attention being recognized for the suit. In other words, my resume. My capacity to look "together." Meaning that I've done my best to not be the one with the black eye. And when I do that, I miss the blessing.

Extraordinarily, blessing begins quite simply...with the affirmation of my name (black eye or no).

Mother Teresa once told a roomful of lepers how much God loved them. She told them that they are "a gift to the rest of us."

Interrupting her, an old leper raises his hand, and she calls on him.

"Could you repeat that again?" he asks. "It did me good. So, would you mind; just saying it again."

Yes. It did me good. Just say it again, please.[4]

We easily forget, don't we, the cathartic power of grace? Which takes us back to a necessary affirmation: We are wired for sufficiency. It makes me wonder whether we trust our own goodness. Deep down I know that people tell me their story because there's a shortage (or an absence) of mercy in their lives. They don't need answers or advice or for me to make things tidy. They—as do we all—need the boundary of grace. They need a blessing. Maybe we protect ourselves from it. Is it hard to admit that we need it?

Speaking of messiness, my face doesn't look so good. Even so, I was blessed this week. Given the permission to be, without the need for absolute certainty. Or answers. Or tidiness. Or striving. Not for what I've done or failed to do. To be just Terry.

● ● ● ● ●

Have you heard of the Church of the Exceptional? It's a nondenominational, interracial ministry devoted to ministering to the physically and mentally handicapped in the area around Rutherford County, North Carolina. In 1974, then-Governor Jimmy Carter and Dr. Norman Vincent Peale were invited to present a *Guideposts* award to the congregation, where thousands had assembled in a municipal center in Georgia. Before the speeches were delivered, the liturgy called for the lighting of the main altar candle.

A middle-aged woman with Down syndrome walked slowly but proudly down the center aisle carrying a lighted taper. The pastor followed closely, to offer assistance. They reached the altar, but despite repeated efforts, the candle would not light. The crowd held its breath, and Carter recalls a sense of embarrassment that welled up inside. The pastor moved forward to help, but she shook her head, and continued to try. Finally, the candle was lit, and the crowd erupted into applause. But the brightest thing in the huge auditorium was the woman's face, which glowed with happiness.

Jimmy Carter writes in his book *Our Endangered Values* that he doubts whether anyone that night remembers his words. But every life was affected and touched by this woman's faith and determination.[5]

In my mind, I am still in that municipal center, watching as she lights one candle — undaunted and steadfast — this heartwarming glow spilling person to person throughout the gathering. And now into my study here on Vashon Island. Yes. I need stories to remind me that grace and hope, and savoring and gratitude, and courage and resiliency are alive and well. The catch, of course, is that these fountains of grace are not necessarily where we expect to find them.

Here's what I think: The woman is not just lighting a candle, but inviting all of us to a paradigm shift. A different way of seeing. A different way of being. A different way of loving. Most of us seem to have an aversion to anything "broken" (especially our own brokenness, speaking of obstacles). Still wedded to the notion that those who are different need to be marginalized or "fixed." Which means that we make premature judgments, naming whatever is wounded or shattered or broken, as wrecked or ruined or threatening, and to be feared; and we miss—we do not see—the flame and the glow of the glory of God that is within each and every one of us.

What is it about labels that seduce us? Or do they comfort us? There is no doubt that fitting life (and people) into boxes is easier. We are certain we know. We are certain we are correct. And it does tidy things up a bit.

It's just too easy to fuel the fire of misunderstanding and intolerance and small-mindedness when I witness all of this through the lens of my own labels. I can literally imagine myself sitting on that platform, thinking, "Why in heaven's name are we letting this woman light the candle? Is there not an easier way? How did she get to be one of us?"

I do know that when we label, we exclude, rather than include. Not only individuals, but encounters too. I do know that when we label, we live with scotoma, which means selective blindness. And scotoma shuts down our heart, our capacity to care, give, love or welcome.

You believe WHAT?
What are THEY doing here?
What can I receive from THEM?
Why should I help THEM?

More often than not, Tion Medon's counsel to Obi-Wan Kenobi on Utapau (for Star Wars aficionados) is right on: "There is no war here unless you brought it with you." For starters, Lord knows the world could use a little more tenderness right now. I live on an island. And I would be fibbing if I told you I didn't want to put my fingers in my ears, hum loudly, and pretend the news and the world would go away. But then I read a story of a woman's resilience carrying a candle of hope.

I can tell you that in the church of my youth, I was weaned with an aptitude for intolerance. We knew exactly whom God didn't care for. Who was on the outside looking in. And we made no bones about naming names. We shunned people. We damned them to hell. When I grew up, I knew in my heart it wasn't right, but I confess that under the guise of walking the fine line, I stayed silent too long. I cannot do that anymore. I know what fear can do. And I don't want to live that way. I don't regret any choices I have made, but I do regret the things I didn't do. When I chose not to speak out, I was wrong, because I read the faces of the crowd to see what placates.

St. Francis is helpful here. Simply, Francis was a heartfelt ally to everything and everyone around him. He began with this assumption, from man to beast, from the trees to the stones, from the sun to the moon to the changing seasons; each is kindred spirit. As kindred spirits, he believed that mankind would naturally be drawn to honor acts out of love and respect, rather than anger, exclusion and supremacy.[6]

What I am learning is this: Perhaps the very people I exclude, the ones who carry the light—who carry the candle—are the ones that invite me to savor the moment and live in the present. They will allow me to see the Grace of God. And the expansive reach of God's acceptance. To every single one of us. Whether I like it or not, it seems that the kingdom of God will be radically and scandalously inclusive. Think of that. God loves broken people and people who have been marginalized and downtrodden and who don't fit into boxes. God loves infidels, idiots, the shunned and the heathen. Now that, that is one radical hospitality. That is truly a Church of the Exceptional.

This is good news: Grace cannot be confined or contained or constrained. We don't dole it out to the deserving. We spill it…to anyone and everyone. And one lit candle makes a difference.

I will choose to live wholeheartedly from the Gospel of Grace for all, which may mean leaning into untidiness and discomfort, and a willingness to be honest about what makes it uncomfortable for me.

So. How then shall we live?

This is important. *Not,* how then shall we react? That's different altogether. Sputtering and muttering and harrumphing never wears well. Back to the Church of the Exceptional: the woman is my teacher. In persistence we choose steady, daily acts of gentleness and kindness and inclusion and healing. One foot in front of another. It's not just about belief. Heroes live the sacrament of the present. Heroes are ordinary souls who carry the weight of ordinary life. And heroism is born in every act of kindness and compassion and inclusion, no matter how small. Because in a world cynical and afraid, it takes courage to be kind and generous of spirit, and to fight for mercy and justice.

Today, time in the garden. The garden detoxifies me. We are still not free from a possible winter freeze, but the signs of new life everywhere make me grin and giggle. And Lord, that does my heart good.

Try This

Look around your house, your yard, your office. What are the messages our culture gives us about the necessity of a tidy life? What are we told about untidiness? Or disarray? And why do we seem to put a moral price tag on it? As in…once you tidy up or straighten out or get mended, you can start living your life.

SECTION TWO

• • • • •

What Gets in the Way?

Chapter Five

What Blocks Our Light?

Should you shield the valleys from the windstorms, you would never see the beauty of their canyons. — DR. ELISABETH KÜBLER-ROSS

John D. Rockefeller was once asked, "How much money is enough?" And he answered, "Just a little bit more."

Courage is not the absence of fear, but rather the judgment that something else is more important than fear. — AMBROSE REDMOON

This little light of mine, I'm gonna let it shine," we sang passionately as children, our index fingers swaying. "Let your light shine," Jesus said in Matthew's Gospel. But here's the deal: Jesus never said, "Make the light." Jesus never said, "Be good at light shining. Or even, join the light shining committee at your church." He said simply, "Let," meaning allow, meaning get out of the way, because the light is already inside of you. And yet, for whatever reason, we don't think of ourselves as light-shining material.

"Put it under a bushel, NO," we sang, "I'm gonna let it shine."

Here's what I do know; when we give in to fear or victimhood or resentment or the assumption that we're shining the light to win someone's approval, we put a bushel over the light. And that never works out so well…Meaning that we are no longer at home in our own skin, literally giving our identity over to something unrecognizable.

We are born to savor. Yes.

We are wired to be present. Yes.

We live the sacrament of the present moment, obstacles and all.

Even so, we find ways to put that light under a bushel. And, the bushel always blocks the light.

In this section, we will talk about three paradigms that derail us, three paradigms that become bushels, blocking the light. A paradigm is the lens through which we see and navigate the world around us. And we will talk about the invitation to make a paradigm shift. Because when our current paradigm is inadequate, these ingredients—diversion, if only, perfection—derail us.

"I love the idea of practicing and embracing the sacrament of the present moment, but what do I do with all the bunkum that gets in the way? I must be missing something," wrote one participant in one of my workshops. I give her five stars for the word *bunkum*.

Bunkum. Let's just call it a technical term. Bunkum is anything that clogs, congests, obstructs, derails, hinders, impedes, frustrates or complicates. There is no moral price tag here. Bunkum (whether neutral or toxic) rains on the parade of our well-being. Because of bunkum, we give our energy to worry or stress or anxiety, meaning anything other than the moment. And here's the irony: Bunkum can do its thing even in the middle of the good stuff. You know, our necessary and constructive efforts to do good. Think of Jesus's ministry with crowds, his service, and his commitments. And yet, at some point, he needed to say NO.

I can say from my own experience that there is such a thing as too much good, as it is easy to become weary with well-doing. Now we call it compassion fatigue. The point here is that even in "well-doing" I can be somewhere other than where I am right now, that even in my "well-doing" I can miss the present moment.

It is important for us to name the bunkum. We will take a look at each of the three paradigms—diversion, if only, and need for perfection—and be honest about the power each has to remove us from being present.

Bunkum neutralizes NO. I say yes when I mean no. Or, I say yes even though I know it will be detrimental. Bunkum neuters our yes. Bunkum recalibrates my value. In other words, I'm somebody because of my busyness, or my service, or my stuff, or my sway, or even my victimhood.

When plaque (bunkum) accumulates, flow is restricted. We are no longer lighthearted, vital, relaxed, animated, or upbeat. In other words, we live with barriers. Bunkum restricts the artery of wellbeing. Through this artery pulses lightheartedness and gladness and joy and rejuvenation and compassion. And the gifts from the sacrament of the present—savoring and gratitude—keep that artery open.

St. Francis knew all about bunkum. And the pivotal moments in his life are an emphatic NO to bunkum. During his youth, Francis was not in want for "stuff" or distraction or if only. There are plenty of stories about a spoiled boy who indulged himself with fine food, wine, and wild celebrations. By age fourteen he had left school, and become known as a rebellious teenager who partied, drank frequently and broke the city curfew. It didn't hurt him that he was known not only for vanity, but for charm. Francis's father was very wealthy and owned a substantial textile business. And Francis was expected to follow in his father's footsteps. It is not surprising that cloth-trade life bored young Francis. He had other dreams, "if only" dreams; say, a future as a knight, a medieval action and war hero.

It was not long after his encounter with a leper he passed on the road, after he intentionally embraced that which nauseated him, hugging and kissing the man, when he confronted his need to say no to bunkum. And to say yes to living present, front and center in his life. And to say yes to the light that shines from within.

He begins to dress in rough clothing, and he begins to make new choices. He takes precious merchandise from his father's store and sells it in order to pay for the rebuilding of a fallen-down chapel. He also sells his father's horse. This didn't go over very well. Francis's father, Peter Bernardone, would have preferred the other Francis, wearing fancy attire and throwing parties for his buddies. It's one thing to wear rough clothing, but it's another to learn that your son spent his time caring for the lepers, who were living in the valley below Assisi.

There's a vivid scene. Peter, boiling with rage, drags Francis before the bishop of Assisi and demands the return of his property and goods. Francis readily agrees to this. And then, in the hearing of all present, Francis said, "From now on I will no longer say, 'My father, Peter Bernardone,' but 'Our Father who art in heaven.'" Francis gave back to his father not only his property and goods, but the money and all his clothes as well. Francis then removed his own clothing, and carefully placed it on the ground.

The bishop, admiring Francis's fervor, drew him into his arms and covered him with his mantle. The bishop understood that Francis's actions were inspired by God—and were part of God's way of leading Francis into an amazingly new form of life. Francis's heart was overflowing with gratitude and joy. His heavenly Father had set him free of all attachment to earthly things—free from bunkum, if you will. And his light spills to us still today.[7]

I can tell you that I don't have much fancy attire to rid myself of, but I do have bunkum nonetheless, so it's just a question about where to begin. It's so easy to give in to our compulsion to be cerebral and to make a list to solve the conundrum. We live in a world attracted to any workshop or book on bunkum elimination. Or perhaps, even better, bunkum management skills.

However, let's pause here. This is important: Embracing and understanding the sacrament of the present moment is not about bunkum elimination. In other words, we are not anti-bunkum. We are pro sacrament of the present moment. And there is a profound difference. As we learned in the previous chapter, one of the most elemental truths about the sacrament of the present is that it is tangible, embraced in the middle of the most ordinary of days. Even in the middle of sorrow. Even in the middle of hardship or adversity. But sometimes we don't understand this truth until we are baptized by circumstance.

Robben Island is famous. It is the South African prison where Nelson Mandela and many others were incarcerated because of their struggle to end apartheid. Mandela served eighteen of his twenty-seven years in prison in Robben Island. The writer Margaret Wheatley tells a story of a time she had the unique privilege of touring Robben Island, now a UNESCO World Heritage site.

The tour group stood in a long, narrow room that had been used as a prison cell for dozens of freedom fighters. Picture yourself in a space crowded, cramped, and barren. The prisoners lived without cots or furniture, cement floors for a bed. The only light entered through slender windows near the ceiling.

The tour group listened to the guide's narration. "I was a prisoner in this very room," he tells them. The gravity of his words mingles with the cold seeping up through the floor.

There is a chill. The group stares through prison bars, surveys the lifeless cell, and tries to imagine suffering from relentless threats and capricious brutality.

The guide pauses, as if remembering, gazing the length of his former cell. Speaking quietly, almost a whisper, he says, "Sometimes, to pass the time here, we taught each other ballroom dancing."[8]

When I first read Wheatley's story, I wasn't ready for that ending. Even with the gut-wrenching bleakness, I confess to grinning, and then laughing out loud. Ballroom dancing? A group of demoralized and weary men, beaten down and brutalized, teaching one another to dance. You gotta love it.

So yes…even in a place where there is severe bunkum, we still have a choice; we can embrace the sacred. Even in rough waters, we can still dance with manatees.

Yes, we know that it is wiser to light a candle than to curse the darkness. But let's be honest. Sometimes life is dark, and it is not fun. Grief is real. Adversity is real. Life can be cruel. People can be crueler. Suffering happens. Suffering hurts. We reach a tipping point. And prison walls are made of real concrete. And finding a candle is not always easy, let alone the motivation to light it.

This is why I love the Robben Island story. It is so counterintuitive. It is about a paradigm shift.

Let me get this straight: in times of anxiety or fear or suffering or distress—when our equilibrium is catawampus, when we want to go away, or get away from it all…

We are invited to open our heart?

We are invited to dance?

The prisoners in Robben Island would say yes. They would say that in adversity, the medicine of intimacy allows us to become more human; that even times of sorrow or discontent can become fertile ground for generosity of spirit, mystery, delight, savoring, celebrating, presence, touch, connection, tenderness, vulnerability, risk, and—yes—even gladness. I love the story, because it is also a reminder about embracing the gift of sufficiency.

It doesn't make immediate sense to us to live into (or lean into) our vulnerability, to open up to what might happen. I understand. Because our tendency is to give way to caution. To let our heart constrict. To appear tough and self-sufficient. To find safe haven, even if that means shutting down. To, at the very least, find an enemy—stress, obligations, lists. With an enemy, at least there is someone to blame for any muddle.

The irony is that in every choice between openness and self-protection (and they are choices), we relinquish our very ability to choose. Our heart tells us to resonate with this desired sentiment to dance. But now we're back to this hope that someone will provide us with detailed instructions. Or, with a manual: "Proper Manatee Dancing." Because somehow, we do not believe that the dance—the perseverance, the light, the tenderness, the intimacy, and the wholeheartedness—is already within us. It is our DNA. "This little light of mine." We are wired. Yes.

New to both the town and the church, Ellen wanted to be involved, to give of herself, to share her gifts. As it happened, the parish needed a new tapestry for one of the smaller chapels. And as a seamstress, Ellen considered this a perfect opportunity. She worked diligently, using colorful and delicate fabric, recreating a well-known rendition of Mary the Mother of Jesus. Others who had seen it were effusive, affirming that what she had created was beautiful. When the day for the unveiling arrives, Ellen presents her gift with an understandable sense of gratification and fulfillment. The answer from the church committee is unexpected and brief, "We can't use this." Because the tapestry was inappropriate or distasteful? No. "The dimensions of the tapestry," they tell her in a very measured tone, "are not quite correct."

As Ellen tells me her story, I want to laugh out loud, until I realize that she is serious. And I can feel my exasperation with small mindedness. "You're kidding," I say. Then, "I'm sorry. That must have felt crazy."

"At first, I was completely deflated," she tells me. "But some time passed and then it occurred to me; I'm going to be OK. Do you know why? Because I didn't make the tapestry for them."

This is a story about how bunkum—diversion, if only, need for perfection—can change the narrative and can get in the way.

Yes, life can squeeze us.

Yes, circumstances can be unfair.

Yes, people can be cruel and without mercy.

And yes, the "system" can be crippling.

I can assure you that in her situation, I could have found a way to nurse a grudge. But here's the deal: If we don't learn Ellen's lesson, in the end we become encumbered, because we will cede our identity and our power—which means that we give up our ability to choose, to create sanctuaries, to be intentional, to be generous, to be big-hearted, to be empathetic, to be compassionate, to forgive and to be willing to grow and to change, to live fully in the present.

"We live like ill-taught piano students," Robert Capon reminded us. "We are so afraid of the flub that will get us in dutch, we don't hear the music, we only play the right notes."

"Let your light shine," Jesus said, not, "Find the right candle." So, I think of Ellen's story. And I'm glad for the invitation to connect with the core in me, with the light that shines (or at least to understand the reason I put a bushel over it), and to embrace the certainty and savor the gladness that comes when we recognize, honor, and respect the image of God in everyone. No exceptions.

Today, how do we learn what Ellen learned?

For starters, vulnerability is OK. Welcome it. It is a place from which we speak the truth. Don't be afraid.

When we name the bunkum, it has less sway and influence. In the next three chapters, we will be naming and acknowledging what gets in the way.

OK, confession time. This isn't easy for me to write about, because there have been times this year when I have wrestled with melancholy and disheartenment. I have felt empty, in a place where it is easy to believe the whole world is colored by gloom. This I know: When we are given over to fear, we cannot rest, or absorb, or create, or take delight. And it is easy to forget Ellen's poignant wisdom that tapestry-making is about living the sacrament of the present—this present moment—wholehearted, and without need for approval.

> We have the capacity to say yes.
> We have the capacity to be a home for grace, not judgment.
> We have the capacity to be a home for empathy, not intolerance.
> We have the capacity to be a home for compassion, not meanness.
> We have the capacity to be a home for hope, not fear.
> And yes, we have the capacity to dance.

"Never allow a person to tell you no who doesn't have the power to say yes." Thank you, Eleanor Roosevelt.

Here's the other part of Ellen's story. I love this…what started as an obstacle (impediment or hindrance), literally becomes a place from which her world (and mine) is transformed. Let's face it: More often than not, we resist and even resent obstacles. We no longer see the tapestry, but only that which diminishes and belittles and shames. We can feel overwhelmed and it is easy to be jaded. It is so easy to quit. But what if beautiful tapestries are born in these very places where we are ready, literally, to give up?

So, where do we find this reservoir that gives us the courage and strength and spirit to move forward? I can tell you that overcoming obstacles is not the goal. As if we must "defeat" someone or something. Lord help us. Ellen's story is not about who "won" or "lost." It is about being at home in your skin and living from your whole heart in this present moment. It is about knowing that each day, we are able to continue to weave the tapestry of our lives with a purity of spirit and intention.

Let us be that place of affirmation.

This is our invitation to pay attention to the certainty that each of these bunkum ingredients depletes us. And the certainty that every one of us needs the permission to feed (or fill) the reservoir that is already there. Not hearing the music while nursing our fear of missing the right notes. And fear becomes a taskmaster. It hits me that the tapestries I create are no longer about what is in my heart, but about who I need to please or impress or even amaze…or just irritate. Notice Ellen's paradigm shift: It's not just choosing to create the tapestry, it's that we choose to give up being afraid…of not being enough, of not measuring up, of being judged as insufficient.

This past week, summer solstice, our longest day. I savored every moment. This weekend, the Vashon Island Garden Tour, exquisite gardens to wander and relish and point…and envy. I'm on the patio tonight, enjoying a wee dram, watching the birds, and letting the gift of ordinary days wash over me.

Try This

What is the difference between being anti-bunkum, and pro-sanctuary? What are ways that we can be pro-sanctuary—creating places where mindfulness, grace and the power of the present are alive and well?

Chapter Six

Diversion

By means of a diversion, a man can avoid his own company
twenty-four hours a day. —Blaise Pascal

I was running past the high: hurrying past the very transcendent
moments I was seeking. —John Jerome

Diversion is the default hobby of our day. Diversion is anything
that is intended to take our attention away from noticing,
focusing, being present. And here's the deal: Undivided is
precisely what attention is not. Diversion always gets in the way of
the savoring the present. Diversion is exacerbated in a world where
multitasking is considered a spiritual gift. In a world where busy is
considered an enviable status and even a compliment. "How are you?"
"Never been busier." "Wow. Lucky you."

In a world where hurry feels good, diversion exaggerates hurry. Let's
be honest, it feels good to go fast. But at some point, the speed of
life, the daily fire hydrant of data takes a toll. To put it in perspective,
according to research by Roger Bohn of the University of California,
San Diego, if you combine mobile phones, the Internet, e-mail, televi-
sion, newspapers, books, social media, etc., we receive every day about
100,500 words (or 23 words per second) during our twelve waking
hours. These are just numbers, I know, but when you add it all up, it
means that we are receiving 34 gigabytes of information per day, on

average. I'll give you a hint: That number is OK for a computer, but it's not so good for a human.

We all can see that magnitude lures us to hurry. And hurry is seldom fruitful. I love Henry David Thoreau's comment, "The man whose horse trots a mile in a minute does not carry the most important messages."

It is no surprise, then, that hurry exaggerates worry. We live in a world that trucks in worry.

Do you think your life is OK? Think again.

Do you think you're happy? Think again.

Do you think you are content with your...(fill in the blank) cellphone? Perfume? Breakfast cereal? Think again.

Our Madison Avenue culture peddles this brew, mixed with a splash of distraction, with options for seductive rabbit trails. The result of this intoxicating beverage? Our identity is being questioned and tested incessantly. And more often than not, we come up short. (Here's a tip: If you want to sell anything in our Western culture, make the person feel like they are being left behind.) The effectiveness of diversion is predicated on the assumption that following the rabbit trail will make things OK.

This works, until we are undone, gratefully, by a sacrament.

A first grader walked through the garden chasing a rabbit and stopped in her tracks when she realized she was standing in the middle of the flowers. "It looks like magic!" She said as she spun around in awe.

For a moment, her world stood still. A reminder for all of us to stop the merry go round and allow time for those moments of awe! *Thisness.* That's the secret. She stopped.

I wrote *The Power of Pause* in part as an invitation for the necessity to do one thing at a time. When we pause, we see. So, I wonder, did you pause today? If you did, I hope you were undone by a sacrament.

What did you see that made your heart glad?

"To be calm becomes a kind of revolutionary act," Matt Haig writes in *Reasons to Stay Alive.* "To be happy with your own non-upgraded existence. To be comfortable with our messy, human selves, would not be good for business." We live in a commodity (transactional) world, invested with making us other than who we are. And we may not even perceive ourselves as confined by this paradigm of scarcity (or non-presence).

A four-year-old boy says to his momma. "Momma, momma, listen to me. But this time, with your eyes." We are born to savor. We are wired to be present. And yes, we concur. Wholeheartedly. "Count me in," I say hearing the four-year-old's request. But that's where the sticky wicket persists. Diversion elbows in. And too often, something internal goes off the rails.

It doesn't hurt that I carry my diversion device (my cell phone) with me wherever I go. And social media breeds FOMO (fear of missing out) and comparison to other lives. We eagerly scan postings that leave us wondering if we are enough. I'm smiling, because I sound like my father's generation, lamenting the advent of technology and computers and the end of civilization as we know it. Lord have mercy. So, I'm not here to demonize, but to invite us to be present, just as the little boy invited his mama, to listen with our eyes. To do that, we need the permission to slow down, to say no to diversion as the narrative for our day. Or, to heed Gandhi: "There's more to life than increasing its speed."

"It's been a rough day," a young woman tells me after a workshop on creating places of sanctuary in our life. "And I'm not in a good place. Because none of my 'tools' are working."

Rough days we all know. All too well. But the non-functioning or insufficient "toolkit," that's never fun. These tools are the aptitude or capability we use to handle and cope and navigate. Yes. I do understand. I know what that feels like, when inside everything is unsightly or discouraging or dark—even to the point of hopelessness. Interestingly, what rocks our boat is not just being in a "bad place," so much as the realization that we are certain (at least at the time) that we have no resources to handle it. Or the tools that worked so consistently in the past just up and quit. (Which makes me wonder, is there a warranty on coping skills? Or perhaps a possible refund?)

"That puts us in a pickle," I tell her (after a good bit of silence). "You have no tools. And I, unfortunately, have no answers for your questions. I do, however, have a story."

"Life," Lucy tells Charlie Brown, "is like a deck chair."

"Like a what?" asks Charlie Brown.

"Like a deck chair. Some people put their deck chair at the front of the ship so they can see where they are going. Some people put their deck chair at the rear of the ship so they can see where they've been. On the cruise ship of life, Charlie Brown, which way is your deck chair facing?"

"I haven't figured out how to get mine unfolded yet." says Charlie Brown.

"And guess what?" I tell the young woman. "It's OK for us to begin there."

Which is another conundrum—'fessin' up. There are times when we know we have a folded deck chair or we know our tools are not working, but surely there's no need to let on. "What would they think?" If you add weakness and vulnerability to broken coping skills, it's a lethal elixir spawning this penchant we have for inherent unworthiness (inculcated by our culture). And down the rabbit trail we go.

There's a great story about one particular shrine in medieval England. The shrine is said to have granted miracles to any married couple of long-standing who had never wished themselves unwed.

How many miracles were ever recorded at that site? None, actually. There is, of course, no reference to this mythical religious site, but to my mind, it should have existed. Not that anyone would have visited. Or 'fessed up. Although there is not a single one of us who, in our secret hearts, didn't imagine walking away from it all at some dark time in our journey…you know, when the tool kit quit working.

Even knowing all of this, we still want someone to discover the newer and better tool kit (and, if possible, put it on sale). That's just it. We live in a world wired to "fix" whatever is "broken." I saw an ad for a new cell phone that promised, "Designed for Serious Multitasking!" This made me laugh out loud, because, apparently, if we're going to multitask, it had better be "serious."

When we fixate on the right tools, we miss the point that what we are looking for is already inside us. And the holy thing that is inside of each of us is that which stirs and arouses the search in the first place. After all, "You can't buy it, lease it, rent it, date it or apply for it," Anne Lamott reminds us.

In our *Let's Make a Deal* world (Door #1? or Door #2?), it's not just that we don't find it—whether it is peace of mind or love or well-being or savoring the present—it's that we don't even recognize it when we see it. Let alone celebrate it. Or, it is possible that what's behind Door #2 is not what we expected it to be…say, an empty tool kit.

Here's the other conundrum. We're invited to pause, to slow down. But pausing is not our first choice. This isn't surprising given our tendency to be consumed by bunkum, or all that is wrong with our lives and world. So, we give our energy to the diversion of problem solving. What preys on our mind, when we are updating our Facebook statuses, are the things that we assume we need to figure out and then solve. With enough distraction, I think we hope that we can keep negativity at bay.

• • • • •

"This is one of our fears of quiet; if we stop and listen, we will hear this emptiness," Wayne Muller writes. "But this emptiness has nothing at all to do with our value or our worth. All life has emptiness at its core; it's the quiet, hollow reed through which the wind of God blows and makes the music that is our life. Without that emptiness, we are clogged and unable to give birth to music, love, and kindness."[9]

•   •   •   •   •

"All of humanity's problems stem from man's inability to sit quietly in a room alone," wrote Blaise Pascal. It is no surprise then, that in our world, diversion is a drug of choice.

Holy Now is one of my favorite Peter Mayer songs, with its message of the holiness of everything.

Yes. I know. It's all well and good on paper or in song. But what about real life? John Duns Scotus (a Franciscan theologian in the thirteenth century) talked about "thisness," the particularity of the Most Extraordinary Ordinary Thing in the World. *Thisness* reminds us that being present is not about arriving at some Zen state of mind. And being present is not about dismissing what is current. Being present is about honoring precisely what is current—which means the wonderful scandal of the particular. Our mind is more pleased with universals—those never-broken-always-applicable rules and patterns that allow us to predict and control things. Well, such rules may be good for science, but they are lousy for life.

So, how do we honor "thisness"? We start by understanding that thisness is the real deal.

For starters, here's the good news: We have no need to run from moment to moment. Or from any possibility of being misunderstood or flawed. Or run from what we should have or should not have done sooner _____(fill in the blank).

Did you know that every day the Wright Brothers went out to try their new "flying machine" they would take five sets of parts? They did so because that's how many times they would crash before they came in for supper.

Remember in chapter four when we talked about the sacrament of the blessed present as alive and well, obstacles and all? In other words, there is no protocol or script. For the Wright Brothers, crashes were a part of the journey. And these crashes were not at all objectionable or unpalatable. The Wright Brothers practiced the sacrament of the blessed present crashes. Who knew?

I'm glad to learn from my friend Phil Volker. (I wrote about him in my book *Sanctuary: Creating Space for Grace in your Life*). After Phil learned he had stage-4-cancer, he decided he wanted to walk the Camino de Santiago in northern Spain. His doctor was not effusive about this plan, for good reason. This didn't stop Phil. So, before he received his doctor's permission to go, he began the journey walking on a half-mile path cut through the acreage surrounding his house on Vashon Island. By the time his doctor said OK, Phil had logged five hundred miles on his island Camino.

In the film *Phil's Camino*, a compelling documentary about his physical and spiritual journey, Phil says, "So initially when you get cancer, you're striving to be cured and that's what doctors do, they cure you. But I've discovered that there's a difference between being cured and being healed. Being cured is being over your disease. To me right now at this point, I'm striving to be healed, which means that you're reconciled with the bigger picture. You're reconciled with God and your family and all the important things. So, whether you're cured or not is sort of secondary."

Today, Phil still walks the "Camino," on the path cut through the acreage surrounding his house. But now he walks with all sorts of visitors (fellow journeyers) who come from hither and yon to join him.

Which brings us full circle back to the tool kit. Whether stuff gets "fixed" or not, is secondary. This resonates with me. The way that diversion focuses on the rabbit trail of being cured. And when diversion wins, we miss the healing.

"Everything is holy now," is the deep end of the scandal of the particular. And it will always eclipse an empty tool kit. In the scandal of the particular, we walk, sing, eat, savor, adore, listen, feel, relish, taste and love. We savor. Or, we sit silent.

Illustrious painter Andrew Wyeth admired Edward Hopper. Wyeth enjoys telling of a party after an opening at the Metropolitan Museum of Art. Wyeth and Hopper were invited to a cocktail party on a penthouse terrace. Abstractionists Stuart Davis and Jackson Pollock were talking techniques and philosophies. Hopper, off to one side, suddenly tapped Davis on the shoulder and said, "Very interesting and I'm sure you're right. But can you boys deny that?" He gestured out at the glowing tones of the setting sun striking across a skyscraper. "Everybody was silent," remembers Wyeth. "That was it. There was nothing they could say."

We live with, and from, our whole heart.

● ● ● ● ●

August means we start to think about summer leaving us here in the Pacific Northwest. It's hard to savor the flowers when we're diverted, chasing the rabbits of what if and if only. I walk my garden, playing mental games over the summer project list in my mind, wondering why I accomplished so little. A pair of goldfinches clamor and prattle at the feeder. And a regal guest stops by the pond...a great blue heron, with its long bill, neck, and legs, graceful and elegant. He stands still, waiting for prey to blunder by. I'm smiling ear to ear, and like the little girl, can't stop saying, "It looks like magic." A good reminder to put my list down. And remember the wisdom of the little boy, "Momma, momma, listen to me. But this time, with your eyes."

Try This

Find a place where people are in a hurry. Now, sit and watch, not to judge, but to notice what happens when hurry / busyness consumes us. Is there anyone who is not in a hurry? What does hurry (or the sense of hurry) make you feel? How long does it take to let go of the hurry?

Chapter Seven

If Only and Someday

Contentment. I'm 24 and have never known it. Forever in pursuit and don't even know what I'm chasing. — HAROLD ABRAHAMS (in *Chariots of Fire*)

Sister Lychen had a word of prophecy every Sunday in her Pentecostal Church. She'd stand up and say, "The Lord has revealed to me that I will be caught up in the clouds of glory." Every week, the same prophecy.

Eugene's parents would make him take Sister Lychen a plate of cookies, and when he'd get to her house, he would find all the blinds down, and all the shutters closed. Old Sister Lychen lived in a house of gloom. She was waiting to die. Eugene Peterson writes that Sister Lychen represents a brand of Christian faith where life here and now is just a trial, so that life can really start in heaven. You know, someday.

Eugene had a fantasy of bursting into Sister Lychen's house, opening all the window blinds, and saying, "Sister Lychen, look! There's a whole world outside! There's a world of turtles and hummingbirds and hawks and grizzly bears."

You gotta smile…

Although, if we're honest, we'll admit that we all have some shutters or blinds somewhere in our mental house. It's our way of waiting for someday.

Lord knows there's a plethora of cheerleaders (with can't-miss advice or products) who find great motivation in lists, and will give (or sell) me a list of things I need to do to find inner peace, and live in the moment. There's the whole idea of having a "bucket list," those things we want (or need or feel compelled) to do before we die.

In a small bookstore (one of my favorite ways to spend an afternoon, by the way, is holed up in a bookstore), I saw a book called *10,000 Things to Do Before You Die*. I had just started my own list, with only three things on it, so the number 10,000 made me a little dizzy.

The book's lure stayed on my mind for a week or so. So, I did what needed to be done: I sat down on the back patio and watched my cat play near the stream, apparently unaware of any pressure about a list of things to complete before cat heaven. While he's at play, I sit, mouth agape, because a kingfisher honors us with his presence and charisma—this elusive, noble, and elegant bird, parking himself on a limb near the pond, hoping for lunch. Nothing struck his fancy, so after ten minutes or so, he moved on. I guess the good news is that for a chunk of time I didn't care one whit about any list to check off that would make my life complete.

The hitch in our giddy-up is that we're wired to consume, add on, scurry, and expand. Like the rich man in Luke's Gospel:

> "What shall I do? I have no place to store my crops." Then he said, "This is what I'll do. I will tear down my barns and build bigger ones, and there I will store my surplus grain. And I'll say to myself, 'You have plenty of grain laid up for many years. Take life easy; eat, drink and be merry.'" (Luke 12:16–19)

When the goal of living in the present is just another conquest (what we attain, buy, achieve), we are like (to borrow from Meister Eckhart) a man riding an ox, looking for an ox to ride. But hey, if you're a list maker, more power to you. Just do me a favor. Don't make it so heavy it weighs you down. It'll make you walk funny.

However, I guess if push came to shove, I could make a list. Let's start simple. Let's make it three things.

One. Practice the prayer suggested by a Buddhist monk, "If I should wake before I die…"

Two. Today, savor just one moment. Just one. (Who knows…if you let it stretch, you can make it the whole day).

Start here: Sit still and let the other stuff go. If you're lucky, a kingfisher (or turtle or hummingbird or hawk or grizzly bear, or, perchance, a manatee) may stop by. You see, if rest is woven into the fabric of our very selves, then Sabbath is the Creator's invitation to take pleasure in, to recreate, dance, celebrate, enjoy, and absorb this gift called life. An invitation to enter into, to be present in, this life, without the need to complete the list for the life yet to be.

I just finished a great book—Lewis Hyde's *The Gift: Creativity and the Artist in the Modern World.* These encounters or connections (whether our art or our work) are called gifts because they cannot be treated as a commodity: hoarded, bought, or traded. These gifts can only be given, bestowed, offered, shared, and spilled.

"This little light of mine" is always on the move, lightening the load of fellow travelers and opening blinds that have been closed for far too long.

Now, I'm so worked up, I've already forgotten number three on my list. At dinner I ask for input. Any ideas about being so focused on our bucket list we miss the moment? "Pass the blackberry cobbler," my son says. At least I tried.

Later, Zach brings me the book *The Three Questions* by Leo Tolstoy. "Here Dad, this might help." In the rewrite by Jon J. Muth, a boy named Nikolai thought that if he only knew the answers to three questions, he would never stray in any matter:

> What is the best time to do each thing?
> Who are the most important people to work with?
> What is the most important thing (the right thing) to do at all times?

In Tolstoy's version the emperor issued a decree throughout his kingdom announcing that whoever could answer these questions would receive a great reward. Many who read the decree made their way to the palace at once, each person with a different answer. A hermit stood up and looked at the emperor. "But your questions have already been answered."

"How's that?" the emperor asked, puzzled.

"Yesterday, if you had not taken pity on my age and given me a hand with digging these beds, you would have been attacked by that man on your way home. Then you would have deeply regretted not staying with me. Therefore the most important time was the time you were digging in the beds, the most important person was myself, and the most important pursuit was to help me…. Remember that there is only one important time and it is Now. The most important person is always the person with whom you are, who is right before you. The most important pursuit is making that person, the one standing at your side, happy, for that alone is the pursuit of life."[11]

Oh, I just remembered number three: So, I go to my garden, pull a few weeds, and am mesmerized by the cherry tomato plants, chock full. Is there anything like the taste of sun-warmed tomatoes from the vine? I cut some flowers for a living room bouquet: late-blooming roses, black-eyed Susans, and Japanese anemone. It's a warm summer evening, meaning that it is time to sit on the patio, sip a glass of wine, and wait to raise a toast to the full moon (about to rise). Who knows, it may open one of my closed window blinds.

• • • • •

Where does this compulsion or temptation to close the shutters come from? Do we assume some sense of security and control? There is no doubt that we talk about our emotions in a safeguarding way. In other words, we assume that all is safe. Or safer with the blinds down.

Interesting, when my world gets smaller (or I make it so), I assume safety, as if I have control over something. But here's what is so fascinating. Sister Lychen did have control, at least in her mind. However, when she closes the shutters, she trades in her emotional well-being and her capacity for joy and contentment. I'm not so sure that's the kind of control she had in mind.

• • • • •

The middle drawer of Rachel's mother's dresser was filled with silk stockings, dozens of pairs in many exquisite colors, each wrapped in the store's original package. They had never been worn. Rachel admired the stockings, imagining the texture and enjoying the array of colors.

One day she asked her mother, "Why don't you ever wear your silk stockings?"

"Because," her mother answered, "they are too good to wear. They may get torn or damaged. Besides, they are too valuable. It's wartime, and silk is now used for parachutes for our troops. Someday, for a special occasion, I will wear the stockings."

Rachel remembers a family vacation when they were away from their apartment in Manhattan for a month. They returned to a ransacked and burglarized home, their personal belongings askew, scattered and broken. In the main bedroom, the dresser drawers hung open. The middle drawer was completely empty. The silk stockings were gone.

Rachel tells how her father bought more locks for the door. He made certain every house after had at least three locks on the front door.

It is understandable. It is our human instinct, once we've been harmed or hurt, to double-down on precaution.[12]

But Rachel's story is not just about loss, or even about the need for more protection. This is a story about whatever we keep wrapped inside us, awaiting the right occasion. Or moment. Or life. This is a story about if only, and someday. It is as if there's some kind of governor on our emotional life and we either don't want to see, or haven't been given the permission to see what is inside—what is ours to engage or contribute or value or spend? This makes me wonder. What is it that we are waiting for? What experience will rise to the occasion, which will allow us to say, "Now, let life begin?" And when did we swallow the notion that life begins someplace other than where we are right now?

"Eventually I began to use everything I owned," Rachel Remen writes about the lessons she learned. "Perhaps the only way we get to keep anything may be to use it up. Perhaps we are all given many more blessings than we receive."

Perhaps so. May each one of us have eyes to see.

My good friend Bill knows wine. He writes about it, appreciates it, and savors it. He also knows wine people. People with grand and exceptional wine cellars. He told me the story of a couple with one such cellar, a collection to admire. Now mature in age, the couple knew that their years were numbered, and that many of their friends had died with full wine cellars, those rare bottles collected for a special occasion.

"You know," the husband told Bill, "how we say we'll drink it when the occasion is right? And, for some reason, the occasion is never quite right."

So, the couple decided they would collect no more wine. They would enjoy, take delight in, and share the wine that they have. In their words, they decided to "drink their wine cellar."

Count me in. Just tell me how. So, we're back to the magical question. Is there a correct way to do this? Because if I'm going to embrace this present moment—especially in silk stockings, while drinking my wine cellar—I want to make certain that I excel at it!

We need to cut ourselves some slack here, assuming that there is a big prize in spiritual well-being for people who have aced the test on embracing-the-sacred-present technique. Another thing to add to that daily checklist. Something we can cross out with vigor and delight. (Tell me you haven't put things on your list you've already done, just so you can cross them off. Satiating, isn't it?)

I do know this: Savoring the present isn't a beauty pageant. And I have a hunch that people who really do love (enjoy, live, venture, give, risk, embrace) life are literally, unselfconscious about method or practice or performance.

In Rabbi Abraham Heschel's mind, it's even more basic. "I would say an individual dies when he ceases to be surprised. What keeps me alive—spiritually, emotionally, intellectually—is my ability to be surprised. I say, I take nothing for granted. I am surprised every morning that I see the sun shine again."

The great blue heron returned to my garden today. I gawk and grin. He stays for only a short while. This is certain...while he's here, there is no if only.

Try This

I was raised in a culture (religious and social) that told me to tone down joy, to make understatement my default, and to wait until eternal life for all the good stuff. What are the messages we have received (from upbringing—family or religious—and from culture) that reinforce "indefinitely preparing to live"? What are the messages that teach us to shelve emotion? Or assume there's always something better? Or to be apologetic about joy in the very ordinary?

Chapter Eight

Perfection Syndrome — Playing the Right Notes

People say that what we're all seeking is a meaning for life.
I don't think that's what we're really seeking. I think what we're
seeking is an experience of being alive…of the rapture of
being alive. — JOSEPH CAMPBELL

And the day came when the risk to remain tight in a bud was more
painful than the risk it took to blossom. — ANAÏS NIN

S ome movies are worth watching again and again.

In 1979, violinist Isaac Stern visited China. His monthlong
trip is recorded in the Academy Award–winning documentary
From Mao to Mozart. Stern expresses gratitude to the Chinese people
(who issued the invitation for a "cultural visit") telling them that "we
are meeting first as musicians, and then as friends."

Stern collaborates with China's National Symphony Orchestra (the
first American musician to do so), and the film documents Mr. Stern's
rehearsals and performances of Mozart and Brahms violin concertos
with the famous Chinese conductor Li Delun (who also acted as his
guide and translator on his trip).

Yes, the movie touches on the influence of the Western world, and
the lingering effects of the Chinese Cultural Revolution (1966–1976),
which opposed any Western influences and oppressed those who
introduced Western approaches. Isaac Stern comes face-to-face with
the clash between technical skill and artistic interpretation.

The soul of the documentary is the time Stern spends with young Chinese students, coaching, coaxing, teaching and encouraging. The level of their skill is exceptional, and...well, astonishing. A consummate teacher, Stern's task seems to be to inspire them to stop being merely technical masters, and to put their heart and emotion into their playing. With a disarming smile, Stern connects with every student he encounters. He knows that inside each student is not just talent or technique, but a song.

In one tender and inspirational scene, a twelve-year-old girl plays her violin with concentrated and technical perfection (not only to Stern, but to an auditorium packed to overflowing). Stern stops her and says, "OK. Now. Sing the beginning to me." You can hear the translator (trying to find the explanation) and see the look of complete bafflement on the face of the young musician.

"Don't be afraid," Stern says gently. "Don't be afraid. Don't be afraid."

So, she sings, haltingly, the first few bars of the piece.

Stern affirms her after she sings. And says gently, "Listen to the beauty when you sing, naturally flowing from the heart. Now (as an invitation), why don't you play it this way?" She puts the violin to her shoulder and plays lilting and evocative music...no longer just notes.

She gets it. And we get it. It is no longer about precision or technical brilliance ...or making an impression. This is now about what's in the heart.

I have never possessed that kind of technical—musical or otherwise—brilliance. But I do know what it is like to grow up in a world where one lived in fear of letting someone down. I was raised in a church environment where being wrong had eternal consequences.

"Be ye perfect," the Bible told us. Which we interpreted as "without any blemish." Of course, I was not, am not, nor will ever be, perfect.

But then, that's the conundrum. And the implication: Somehow, an imperfect Terry is not enough. I, too, have spent my life trying for concentrated and technical perfection, and I'll give you a hint: It hasn't gone as well as I'd hoped.

Regardless of our background, we're all familiar with these messages that bombard us daily. And they are not subtle. They tell us who we "should" be. They tell us who we are "supposed" to be. The irony is that "they" are in our head, and we're not altogether certain who "they" are. Even so, they tell us that whoever we are, it is not enough. But then...that's the downfall of perfection: Even perfect is never enough. And down another rabbit trail we go.

So, here's the deal: We need to give ourselves the permission to go through a process of unlearning. Perfectionism is not the same thing as striving to do your best. There is a vast difference between perfectionism and living wholehearted. Living wholehearted is built on the promise of sufficiency and enough.

What would it mean to say, "I am enough"? I recognize that there are times I do not honor that Terry, the "it is enough" Terry. Meaning that I do not honor the music that is within this me. There are times when I disavow it, or times when I makes choices that wound (because of fear and vulnerability). Lord knows why, other than some internal need to rain on the parade of our own messy wholeness.

What is your relationship to the need (or is it a temptation) for perfection? Is it treading the water of expectation or a willful blindness or an obligation to please?

The shift begins when we invite a new paradigm about wholeness. So, we do well to heed Parker Palmer's reminder that "wholeness is the goal, but wholeness does not mean perfection. It means embracing brokenness as an integral part of life."

Rachel Naomi Remen, author of the stockings story and a healthy critic of our perfectionist culture (which she calls "a major addiction of our time") writes, "Wholeness is never lost, it is only forgotten. Wholeness is not an achievement, but rather as the reality of being present to who we are, in its entirety, at this very moment."

"There are no shortcuts to wholeness," Palmer again. "The only way to become whole is to put our arms lovingly around everything we've shown ourselves to be: self-serving and generous, spiteful and compassionate, cowardly and courageous, treacherous and trustworthy. We must be able to say to ourselves and to the world at large, 'I am all of the above'."

I do know this...If I am too focused on evaluating (eager for a glimpse of perfection), I cannot embrace the moment—any of it; the joy, the discomfort, the uncertainty, the generosity, the surprises, the pain, the pleasure. If I am measuring and weighing, I cannot marvel at little miracles. If I am anticipating a payoff, I cannot give thanks for simple pleasures. If I am feeling guilty about not hearing or living the music, I cannot luxuriate in the beauty of the heart. The beauty of *my* heart. Putting our arms lovingly around *this* self is an affirmation of St. Francis's reminder that, "All the darkness in the world cannot extinguish the light of a single candle."

● ● ● ● ●

At a recent weekend event, I spent time with a group of spiritual directors, people who are intentional about spiritual wellbeing and mentors to others on their faith journey. I talked with them about the sacrament of the present.

During the Q&A, a man asked, "OK. Help me with this. I practice Centering Prayer and have been faithfully practicing for fifteen years. But I still don't seem to get it. I mean I don't know if I'm achieving the right result. What am I doing wrong? Can you help?"

"Well," I said to him, "that all depends. Are you observing the fifteen- or the thirty-year plan?"

Yes, I confess, my humor is eccentric. I was grateful that everyone in the room laughed. Because every one of us can relate. And I continued, "So, tell me, what on earth makes you think that it's not working?"

You see, when perfectionism (or any kind of perceived perfection) is the goal or end result, every moment, encounter, event, endeavor, prayer, or meditation practice is measured and weighed. "Does this moment pass muster?" Lord have mercy.

Of course this is not uncommon. "I have a lot of people who come in and want to learn meditation to shut out thoughts that come up in those quiet moments," wrote Sara Griesemer, a psychologist in Austin, Texas, who incorporates mindfulness meditation into her practice. "But allowing and tolerating the drifting in our thoughts is part of the process." And every time we find meaning only when we weigh and measure, we too easily miss the collateral beauty in the drifting.

Have you seen the movie *Mr. Holland's Opus*? Glenn Holland spent a lifetime teaching music to a high school band. In one scene, he is giving a private lesson to Gertrude. She is playing clarinet, making noises that can only be described as otherworldly. He is clearly frustrated, as is she. Finally, Mr. Holland says, "Let me ask you a question. When you look in the mirror what do you like best about yourself?"

"My hair," says Gertrude.

"Why?"

"Well, my father always says that it reminds him of the sunset."

After a pause, Mr. Holland says, "OK. Close your eyes this time. And play the sunset."

And from her clarinet? Music. Sweet music.

I returned home to Vashon Island early this morning from Southern California, where I spent a day with a group gathered at St. Paul's Episcopal in Pomona. Our topic: How to be me when the world wants someone else. In other words, do we have the permission, the freedom, to sing the music of our heart?

The sun is shining and it a perfect Autumn day here in the Pacific Northwest, and I smile at how easy it is to play the script: fall is here too soon, or summer went by too fast. And I tell myself that next year, I won't talk that way. Next year, I will savor days like today.

Or I can make the choice not to wait. So, I walk the garden and spend time on the patio. The flowerbeds—still undone from last week's storm—are a muddle. I smile at the great clumps of Japanese anemone, prostrate into the lawn. It's not easy to give up the need for perfection. In my mind, I hear Isaac Stern's gentle urging, "Don't be afraid. Don't be afraid. Just sing the beginning to me."

● ● ● ● ●

A farmer walks along the furrowed row, stopping every three feet, to place a potato start into the soil. His young son keeps pace, on the opposite side of the furrow, weighted with a burlap sack of starts, whole-hearted in assisting his father. He places starts into the soil; unhurried, deliberate, and methodical. There are times when he picks the start from out of the ground, in order to turn it, so that the eye of the potato may be placed at the exact angle.

The neighbor, who has been watching over the fence, decides to offer his opinion. "I see you're planting potatoes," he tells the farmer, "But I'll tell you this; it's going to take you a good long while at your pace. Let me tell you like it is: You'd get it done a whole lot faster if you'd plant this field by yourself."

"Well," replies the farmer, "that may be true, but I'm raising more than just potatoes."

When we live by the narrative that meaning or value is predicated on weighing and measuring, there is more than a reasonable chance we'll be certain that we've come up short. I suppose it is because there are a lot of paradigms that trick us into believing the scorecard is still compulsory, and vital and essential for our identity and wellbeing. I wonder when it happened. I wonder when we started living in a world where being somebody took precedence over just being.

Here's some hopeful news: Letting go of our need for perfection allows us a new perspective (a new lens, our paradigm) for what constitutes success and health and wholeness. My cynical side says, "Sure, that's easy. Just move the bar to underachieving." And I smile. Because savoring, being wholly present, doesn't rest on any laurels or earn medals of achievement. And even my cynical side needs a breather.

After time at the Religious Education Congress in Anaheim, I am in San Juan Capistrano. Outside the rain hammers the roof and patio and the wind howls. I feel like I'm home in Seattle. I've finished three days at the Anaheim Convention Center, glad for the interaction with old friends, and the connection with new friends. But I am sorry I stayed inside, and missed an exquisite and exotic full moon.

Try This

Let's begin by naming notes. The correct notes we assume we need to play. Where does that come from? Why is it so addictive? What are the notes that allure (or addict) you…need to be perfect, fear of failure, need to please, need to impress, shame, fear of inadequacy?

(Always remember that naming is powerful. It takes away some the power and sway.)

Let's talk about our temptation to orchestrate. I see this tendency in education, and we end up teaching to the test. Just teaching correct answers. What are we hoping for when we orchestrate or stage-manage? Hope to (more realistically, expectation to)…Avoid failure or disappointment? Find a way to perfection? Salvage a sense of control?

What happens if we let go of those expectations?

SECTION THREE

· · · · ·

Today I Choose to Honor…

Chapter Nine

Today I Choose...

If it ain't in you, it can't come out of your horn.—CHARLIE PARKER

Everything has already been given. What we need is to live into it.
—THOMAS MERTON

The plain fact is that the planet does not need more successful people. But it does desperately need more peacemakers, healers, restorers, storytellers, and lovers of every kind. It needs people who live well in their place. It needs people of moral courage willing to join the fight to make the world habitable and humane. And these qualities have little to do with success as we have defined it.
—DAVID ORR

In 1905, the sculptor Rodin hired the poet Rainer Maria Rilke as his amanuensis. The result was a strong friendship. One day Rilke confided in Rodin that he had not been writing. That he had some kind of "writer's block." Rodin offered odd advice. He did not suggest anything to do with writing. Or change of diet. Or change of relationship. He told Rilke to go to the zoo.

"What will I do there?" Rilke asked.

"Look at an animal until you see it," Rodin told him. "And two or three weeks may not be enough."

The result? Rilke's *The Book of Pictures*, including the poem "The Panther."

It reminds me of the story told me by a group of retreatants who hiked (divided into smaller groups) through the local mountains near San Diego as a part of their retreat. After the afternoon trek, they eagerly compared stories about which group covered the most ground, and which completed the most demanding hike. Until one young woman asks enthusiastically, "But while you were hiking, did you guys see the eagles soaring over the canyon?" (In other words, what did you see today that made your heart glad?)

The poet Francis Ponge spoke of the "meaning" that is locked in the simplest object or person, and "in these terms, one will surely understand what I consider to be the function of poetry. It is to nourish the spirit of man by giving him the cosmos to suckle."

"What is honored will be cultivated," Plato reminded us. I like that. Not what is believed or printed on a framed value statement. What is honored. You see, to honor means, "to weigh heavy." Beliefs are about nouns. Honoring is about verbs. Because verbs invite and are revealed by actions and choices.

If I don't sit long enough to see, I miss the meaning. Plain and simple. And it's no wonder, since we tend to make seeing or paying attention complicated with our expectations and prejudices that only that which is big or ecstatic or notable or weighty or "spiritual" or "positive" is of value. There must be a payoff. Listen to us: We're always upping the ante on what is never enough.

Every time my mind goes there (you know, "never enough") it makes me wonder whether I trust my own capacity to absorb mercy. In this moment.

Anne Lamott says all one must do in order to hit the reset button is to love mercy. In her book *Hallelujah Anyway*, she describes the experience this way: "Then creation begins to float by, each new day. Sometimes it's beauty, cherries, calm, or hawks; sometimes it's forbearance, stamina, eyeglass wipes, apricots, aspirin, second winds." Fair enough Anne. Thanks for the reminder.

For me, this week, mercy surfaced wrapped slightly different. Morning garden flower surprises that made me giddy, coffee on the patio, YouTube videos that made me cry, a book that invited my spirit to soar, a neighbor cat stopping by to see if our cat (now in heaven) could come out to play, a friend's honest letter that made me say amen, running through the sprinkler—and even, at times, silly phone calls and leaky pipes to repair.

This is an important place to pause, as we begin Section Three. To remind ourselves that not one of the ingredients we choose to honor is an add-on. Or something to be obtained or earned or deserved. Let's remember how we began the book. The sacrament of the present— savoring the present—is in our DNA. Already inside.

So, here's the deal: only in the particularity of the ordinary, the simple, the shadow-side, the uncertain, the vulnerable, the awkward and the small, can life be fully embraced. You see mercy is not found outside the constraints of life. It is discovered and felt and absorbed in the back-and-forth, the ampleness, the messiness, the pudginess of life.

Jim Harrison reminded us, "Paying attention is the only game in town." Paying attention. In other words, to honor. To weigh heavy. Paying attention allows for a holy place to serve the soul. Which makes dancing with manatees a spiritual endeavor and difficult to talk about in this culture because it smacks of some truth reduced to a bumper sticker. But spirituality is another way of saying that life and reality are more than a sum of their parts and more than the answers we deduce from those sums—a good reminder especially for me, whose child-hood world reeked of implied spirituality.

The word *spirituality* has been suspect for some time, conjuring images of those with apparently no real life to live, spending their energies cashing in their coupons for harps on clouds, streets of gold up yonder, and all that. The spirituality we're talking about here, however, is not about a lottery ticket to the next life, but a front-row-center ticket to this one. This life, with its ill-timed meetings, bleating cellphones, financial hardships, demanding children, traffic snarls, and yammering pain-in-the-neck obligations (which are, of course, past due). This life, where once in a while, just for a minute, you stop what you are doing and watch the clouds roll through the southern sky, a conveyor belt of fleece. The wind is out of the southwest, filling your lungs, and you catch a glimpse of a blue heron, taking off from your pond and gliding like a javelin across the sky. This world is now on center stage, no longer peripheral to your duties and obligations. And the full weight of this moment seeps its way back into the grind of the everyday, slowing our heartbeat, giving us a gentler step and a gleam in the eye.[15]

Late in her life, May Sarton was questioned about what she wanted to be when she "grew up."

She replied, "To be human."

Not bad.

• • • • •

About the same time every year, old friends and I gather in Manasota Key, where I was blessed to dance with manatees. And yes, they are old, as in we've been friends a long time—over thirty-five years. And yes, they are old, as in they (like me) take an odd pleasure in getting their AARP discount at the movie theater. We spend the days on a friend's boat, swapping stories, about how life is not easy for some of us—struggles and challenges with kids, or jobs or marriages or expectations—or, all of the above. We don't use our time making a bucket list, but instead, enjoy the days with its endowment of gifts, taking great delight in the little things.

Albert Einstein once said, "Not everything that can be counted counts, and not everything that counts can be counted." That's a good one to bank on. So that's what we do with our days together. We allow ourselves to be enchanted. Giddy at the sightings of soaring manta rays, in awe watching gentle manatees play in the gulf near our boat, silenced in amazement at a family of osprey (mom and dad with four young), imperial and imposing in their nest above the sign that reads, "Manatee Zone. Slow Speed. Minimum Wake."

We point at dolphins and herons and egrets. And enjoy sunsets that make us forget everything on our worry list. Sitting on the beach my friend asked me about my worry list from the year before. "What was on that list? You know, the things that paralyzed you, made you think you wouldn't make it another day?" "I can't remember," I told him. "I rest my case," he said.

When the sun dissolves on the horizon, and the water turns the color of spewed lava, my friend Ed blows a conch shell. It is his variation on a Benedictine compline, a prayer to end the day. We raise our glasses and toast life and these moments of grace.

One night on the boat, we returned from dinner late, well after dark. This is a dicey affair (I had no idea). We were in the Intracoastal Waterway, a stretch along the western coast of Florida from Sarasota to Longboat Key to Manasota Key and Boca Grande, filled with islands and peninsulas, and vast mango groves, looking prehistoric, or like perfect hideaways for a Carl Hiaasen novel. In places the water is shallow, only a foot or so above sandbars. So, traveling after dark is not just an adventure. It can be dangerous (on the shoals and all that, not to mention pirates, although retired Floridians in polyester shorts don't provoke the requisite amount of terror and panic.) Ed's tone is clear, "Watch that red blinking light. Pay attention. We need to stay left of that. If we don't, we're on a sandbar." This is a trip that requires watchfulness. Watchfulness is another good synonym for honoring and weighing heavy.

• • • • •

The husband knew he could not adequately care for his wife, now in the final stages of Alzheimer's. He found a compassionate facility and visited her every day. At noon for lunch. Not 11:59. Not 12:01. Noon. Every day. Until the day of a minor accident when he found himself in an emergency room, his arm being stitched by a nurse as the clock approached the noon hour.

"I need to leave," he said ill at ease.

"Hold on," she told him, "we're not finished here."

"But I must visit my wife at noon," he said.

"Well," she told him gently, "today you can be a little late."

The man told the nurse the story of his wife and of the facility where she lives and how when he visits she doesn't even recognize him, does not know who he is. The nurse patted his hand and said, "That's OK, hon. You can relax. If she doesn't even recognize you, there is no harm in being late this one day."

"No," the man insisted. "I need to go. I need to be there at noon. I know she doesn't recognize me. But I need to be there because I still recognize her."

Invited to guest preach at another parish, Rev. Barbara Brown Taylor asked the priest, "What do you want me to talk about?"

"Come tell us what is saving your life now," he told her.

Taylor writes, "I did not have to say correct things that were true for everyone. I did not have to use theological language that conformed to the historical teachings of the church. All I had to do was figure out what my life depended on. All I had to do was figure out how I stayed as close to that reality as I could, and then find some way to talk about it that helped my listeners figure out those same things for themselves."[14]

To navigate any difficult water in our lives, we need markers. "I need to visit my wife at noon," the man told the nurse. "Everyone needs a sacred place," Joseph Campbell reminds us. This is a non-negotiable. So where is your sacred place? Where are you free to just be? Where you are enough? Where you savor the present? We do not go there merely to fulfill an obligation. We do not go there just to be a good person. We do not go there to impress people we know. We go there because if we don't go, we lose a part of our soul.

That night with my friends, we paid attention to the red light. Because a part of honoring is paying attention to the things that get in the way. We made it to the harbor safely. But here's what I learned: One light at a time. I hope the same for you. What is saving you today?

Today, I will choose to honor…

For me, it is my garden. Yesterday, I had a day between trips. It is a Seattle autumn day, uncertain if it will commit to anything predictable. Clouds move across the sky like sets or props on a grand stage. The breeze rifles through the trees, and a few leaves begin the autumn confetti parade. I tell myself there's work to do, but can't conjure a compelling reason to do it. So, mostly I sit and stare. And for at least a little while…

> I am not phoning.
> I am not blogging.
> I am not tweeting.
> I am not texting.
> I am not emailing.
> I am not mentally editing the to-do list in my head.
> I am resting. And for at least a little while…I am in safe harbor.

• • • • •

I learned a new word: *Sankofa*.

Sankofa (in the Akan language of Ghana), associated with the proverb, "*Se wo were fi na wosankofa a yenkyi*," which translates "It is not wrong to go back for that which you have forgotten."

And there's no doubt that I probably work too hard to make sense of embracing the sacrament of the present. What I really need is a reset button. What I need is *sankofa* time.

Let me tell you a *Sankofa* story about what can happen when we do not honor, or are not at home in our own skin. This is a story about reconnecting with our heart. And the choices we can make that spill to those around us.

Carlton Pearson is a former Pentecostal bishop and TV evangelist. He pastored a megachurch in Tulsa, Oklahoma with over 5,000 members. After a life-altering experience in Rwanda, Pearson had growing feelings that the doctrines he had been taught (and preached) no longer felt true for him. Even so, he believed that he could not allow himself to examine these feelings, mostly out of concern that he would "let down" his congregation. After all, didn't they expect him to supply ready and comforting answers? Would his questioning eventually lead him to abandon his faith? If he were no longer the "preacher with answers," where would he find his identity? Pearson decided, finally, that he could no longer live with the pressure of feeling like a hypocrite, and abruptly left the church.

Alan Lurie writes, "Looking back, Pearson discovered that his reluctance to question the prepackaged doctrines that he had been given, and fear of examining his assumptions about how a man of faith should act, actually diminished his faith and his sense of purpose." Today, Pearson preaches at a new church, where he speaks from his heart and soul without fear of duplicity.

This story is not just about changing a belief system. This story is about what can happen when we live from the core of our authentic self.

Today, I choose to honor...

I can relate to Carlton Pearson. I know the feeling...like an impostor somewhere deep down. Of course, imposter goes with the temptation dangled daily with cultural distractions and rabbit trails for meaning

Every single one of us wants to be at home in our own skin—to live authentic lives. And yet, it is very easy to live from a "false self." For some of us, it happens when we cross an invisible line in the sand of our soul. When our spirit feels finally depleted. When we are fueled only by some need for survival. When we have lost heart because we feel both confused and powerless. When we give in to some default mechanism, always looking over our shoulder to see if we pass muster.

You know the litany. Call it what you like, social acceptance or social routine or public opinion or labeling or a parish "what will they think" group...It all boils down to this: "Who are you going to dance for?" There are so many ways we get derailed. And we create elaborate scaffolding, needed to prop up our glittering image. Or our ego. Or our fear of imperfection. Or our unadorned need to be liked.

It all starts when I buy the myth that this (stuff, achievements, creeds, accoutrements, circumstance) is all there is to my identity. And when I succumb to any contrived or fabricated image, I fall short of my best self. Of that there is no doubt. When I fall short of my best self, I do not speak from my heart. I do not act with compassion. I do not see or honor the common ground we share in this sacrament of the present moment.

True, we live in a world bombarded by messages, that who we are now is NOT enough. At a Catholic parish where I was scheduled to lecture, a woman asked me, "What are you going to talk about?"

"Chocolate and God and the dance of life," I told her.

"But you're not Catholic," she pointed out.

"I quite often feel obligatory guilt," I said, "does that count?"

She scrunched her eyebrows. And continued, "I mean how can you talk about these things if you are not part of the Church?"

I almost told her that I would convert if she bought enough copies of my newest book, published by Franciscan Media, but the irony may have been lost. So instead I said, "OK, I'll make you a deal. Listen to me first. You can try to convert me later, while we're talking and eating chocolate together."

It's easy to allow this hunger for acceptance to seep into our psyche. And if such expectations or labels are not enough, we carry some shame that we should try harder (or at least enroll in a self-help course). We feel undeserving, or under a microscope, or inadequate. Just like the pressure cooker Carlton Pearson experienced.

So. Stop. Literally. Just stop.

There are many mindfulness (meditation and prayer) techniques that teach us to slow down at discomfort and dis-ease. Not to run from it, but to live into it. We make space to ask, to own, to expand, to choose, to invest, to honor. One thing is certain: Without renewal, there is no path to reconnect with our heart again. Yes. So, more than ever we need sustenance—soul food—places of sanity and restoration.

This week I needed to revisit this invitation, to be at home in my own skin. Because I do know this…When I am not at home, I live "at the mercy of": I react. I live defensive. I project. I live afraid. I push people away. I need to label you because you are different and a threat. A contrived script owns me. When that happens, I'm unable to honor (to weigh heavy) those choices that feed my soul.

I know that Pearson's change did not come from just "trying harder." True change only happens when we switch the focus from what is on the outside, to affirmation of what is on the inside.

Richard Rohr reminds us, "Don't push the river." Which is another way of saying, don't get ahead of your soul. The goal isn't to get somewhere. The goal isn't about forcing something to happen. The goal is to be in harmony with the gifts that are already given. The goal is to fall into your life. To fall into this life.

Here's the deal: When we feed the inner life (that part of ourselves that yearns to be connected with something larger than our own ego), there is new freedom to inquire, doubt, question, challenge, connect, forgive, mend, risk, receive, revel, celebrate, restore, and live completely unafraid. And eat chocolate with people who are wonderfully different.

Pausing for contemplation can lead us to reflection and fidelity.

I don't want to pretend that this is easy. (For all our whining about wearing the ill-fitted suit of public opinion, the perks aren't too bad or we wouldn't play along.) Have you read Graham Greene's *The Power and the Glory*? I recommend it. Greene portrays a whiskey priest, who has come to see the light because his own life had become so dark (just like Pearson). To give up our "respectable" image may feel like (or actually be) a fall from grace. But in the end, we embrace the day from an authentic self. The very self that has been there all along.

Rohr again, "Like Jesus, [Saint] Francis taught his disciples while walking from place to place and finding ways to serve, to observe, and to love in the world that was right in front of them." But I can only do that if I'm grounded. Pay attention while walking. Pay attention while living.

Today, I choose to honor...

It's just that too often, our theology feels like a mandatory quiz requiring that we put our life on intermission, in order to make declarations (affirmations about what we believe) that we can now take as CliffsNotes back into life.

Saint Francis invited his disciples, and invites us today:

> To see while we walk,
> To practice gratitude while we walk,
> To savor the day while we walk.

When my garden explodes with bloom and color and gratuitous splendor, there are no words sufficient to paint the tapestry. Not that it makes a difference. Silence is often the best response. To let yourself be carried away. Literally. To rise and swell, and savor and explode, and ride the joy. I don't have the words now, only a good glass of Bordeaux and a good book. The choir (a plethora of birds at the feeder) has begun evensong. Prayer will follow, and I can't wait for the homily, something about the sacrament of the blessed present.

Try This

"Today, I am going to pamper my soul."
—Rabbi Zalman Schachter-Shalomi

Take a break from all those things that invade your soul from the outside world: social media, the 24/7 news cycle, the endless to-do lists. You know what those things are for you. Listen to music, take a walk, read something that feeds your spirit. These are the choices we make that honor our inner being.

Chapter Ten

Welcome Sufficiency; Know the Power of Enough

Where there is Love and Wisdom, there is neither Fear nor
    Ignorance.
Where there is Patience and Humility, there is neither Anger nor
    Annoyance.
Where there is Poverty and Joy, there is neither Cupidity nor Avarice.
Where there is Peace and Contemplation, there is neither Care nor
    Restlessness.
Where there is the Fear of God to guard the dwelling, there no
    enemy can enter.
Where there is Mercy and Prudence, there is neither Excess nor
    Harshness. — St. Francis of Assisi

The older I get, the clearer it becomes to me that no one is cheated
in this world, unless it's by himself, but some of us are so wounded
that we must return to the scene of the crime, must play with the fire
that burned us, must live the scene out as many times as necessary
until it comes out differently. We are not prisoners, no traps or snares
are set about us, but many of us imprison ourselves or at least are
helplessly stalled. — Merle Shain

The opening battle sequence in the movie *Cold Mountain* realistically portrays the gruesome nature of Petersburg's "Battle
of the Crater." Union engineers created a massive crater with
explosives in an attempt to penetrate the Confederate lines. The scene

is a graphic depiction of life's fragile nature. A reminder that there are times and places even in a "Photoshopped" world of atrocity and suffering and cruelty and sorrow.

Before the battle scene, we are introduced to young Oakley, a boy who is helping Inman (the main character of the story) and other Confederate soldiers distributing supplies in the trench. As an aside, Inman comments to a fellow soldier about Oakley's age and that the boy is certainly too young for war. In the battle, Oakley is mortally wounded.

After the battle, a makeshift ER and triage is filled with cots and young bodies (including Oakley), many given whatever comfort that can be afforded in their final hours or minutes. Stobrod—a fiddle player—stands by the bed and begins to entertain (and hopefully console) the boy.

"No," says Oakley, his breathing labored. "Play me something sweet, like a girl is waiting for me."

"You heard him," Inman tells the fiddler.

"I only know a couple of tunes," Stobrod tells them, now ill at ease.

"Like when you're up Bridge's creek," Oakley continues, "and you're thirsty and the water is so cool."

"I don't know what music that is," the fiddler confesses, his face crestfallen. Even so—to grant the dying boy's request—Stobrod puts bow to string and from the fiddle we hear haunting, lilting and evocative music. Music as poetry. Music as a picture to reassure the boy. Music to carry his spirit safely back to Cold Mountain.

"I don't know what music that is."

We are inculcated in a world where there must be a script. Well, that's the part that trips us up. Whether it is happiness or contentment or success or well-being. All we need is the key, the correct information, the right dogma, or, the secret. Tantalizing isn't it? It's easy to be derailed by the notion that information equals control.

But this Cold Mountain story is not about control. This is a story about presence. And our heart. And paying attention. And being in this moment. And welcoming sufficiency. We've all been told to just "let go" or "let it be." And I have told myself to "just chill." Sometimes it helps. Most times, not so much. It's as if it becomes another "thing" on my list. An assignment. You know, "Am I chilling enough?" Just wondering…"Do I need to read a different book about chilling, before I attempt it?"

But here's the deal: Even if I don't know what music that is, I will know it when I hear it, even if I don't have the words. It is the music of sufficiency. It is the music that makes my lungs swell and my heart flutter. There are two aspects of the scene that touch me deeply. One, I am drawn to the vulnerability or openness of the young boy (not only in his acceptance of his "fate," but in not fighting it, or trying to figure it out or blame someone). And two, I am struck and humbled by the transformation in the musician, who "knew" only two songs—until he was invited to the music that is alive and well within his own heart and soul. Music that had, for whatever reason, been dormant or buried or forgotten.

I will confess to you that I too easily play only the two songs I know. I too easily tell myself that the price of playing and feeling the music of sufficiency that is inside of me (multi-layered, authentic, life-giving and heart-rending) may be too steep. I too easily steel myself against anything that can break or rent or tear. I too easily tell myself that if I live that vulnerable and open, it would require too much. I do my best to not let on, but I can live warily and guarded. When I do, I too easily miss the power—and the music—of the sacrament of the present. Music for joy and delight and wonder. Music to quench the thirst of our soul. And music for healing and soothing in those times when life turns abruptly left, and our options seem bleak, and our resolve tank is empty.

I enjoyed Andrew Schulman's book *Waking the Spirit*. Andrew is the resident musician in the Surgical Intensive Care Unit at Mount Sinai Beth Israel hospital in New York. Yes. Musician, in a hospital. Why? Because music soothes. Music heals. Music invites us to remember the power of sufficiency.

So where do we go with Oakley's story? This week, we can all be Oakley, and ask for our song. Or, we can be Stobrod, and put bow to fiddle to soothe and heal those lives we touch. How does this connect us to savoring the present?

Recently, a young man I knew took his own life. We'll never know why, but "life is short, and this time it was bigger than the strength he had…" And I pictured Stobrod with bow to fiddle with the haunting, lilting and evocative music to carry this young man's spirit safely and tenderly back to Cold Mountain and to the angels. It affected me, and I journaled from my heart, looking for music that has been forgotten.

It is Sunday night and I'm dispirited, and not sure how to finish my writing assignment, so I step outside to toast the moon (past half now on a clear azure sky) and sit on the patio for a spell.

And I remember another scene from the movie. When Inman and Ada meet, he wonders aloud if it were "enough just to stand without the words."

"It is," she tells him. "It is."

●　●　●　●　●

Mohini was a regal white tiger. In the 1960s and '70s, she lived at the National Zoo in Washington, DC. Most of those years she lived in the old lion house—a twelve-by-twelve-foot cage with iron bars and a cement floor. Mohini spent her days pacing restlessly back and forth in her cramped quarters, while zoo visitors watched, pointing in awe.

Eventually, biologists and staff worked to move Mohini from such an artificial and cramped environment to a habitat more natural and suitable for her. Mohini's new home covered several acres with hills, trees, a pond, and a variety of vegetation. With excitement and anticipation they released Mohini into her new and spacious environment.

What occurred next, no one expected.

Instead of frolicking in the newfound freedom, Mohini immediately sought refuge in a corner of the compound, where she lived for the remainder of her life. Mohini paced and paced in that corner until, in the end, it made an area twelve-by-twelve-foot, now worn bare of grass.

From the time I was a young boy, my mother told me that the sky was the limit. I could dream or be anything. So why wouldn't Mohini have treasured her freedom? After I read Mohini's story, I had an immediate response, which included a litany of how we too easily live life so small. But it's not that simple, is it? Because over the years, I haven't always seen the cages around me, and I've had a grocery list of "guidance" sermonized at me.

"Do you know what your problem is?"

"Well of course, can't you see?!? All you need to do is…"

"The answer is obvious!"

We can be stuck. No surprise there.

When I travel and talk with people, I hear it frequently. "I feel stuck." Or, "I need a change." I do know this: It doesn't help to have well-intentioned (or worse, self-righteous) people add to the weight of our trance, only to be more driven by "I have to do more to be OK" or "I am somehow incomplete." These "mantras" only reinforce the belief that our life is elsewhere and otherwise, and assuredly, not possible where it is now.

I'll 'fess up. I easily see this "stuckness" in those around me. In myself? Not so much. We may want to love other people without holding back. We may want to feel authentic. We may want to breathe in the beauty around us. We may want to dance with manatees. We may want to sing. And yet…each day we listen to inner voices that keep our life small. In other words, we do stay stuck, imprisoned in ourselves. As if there's a script that includes: "don't, shouldn't, can't be done, what are you thinking? You know that won't work don't you?"

We have internalized the narrative that scarcity is our lot in life. Lord have mercy…Meaning, we end up just like Mohini, pacing in the corner of our domain. Let's remember: It's not the external boundaries that make a difference; it's the internal ones.

This is where we go a bit off the rail. You see, believing our boundaries are external, we seek an external solution—say a whole new environment with hills and a pond and such (or perhaps the addition of a new BMW convertible…just saying). Perhaps the solution is an invitation. "Try this…" If I assume my identity is confined to a cage; I will carry that identity with me wherever I go. I am unable to welcome sufficiency. However, when I learn that my identity is deeper—more profound and remarkable—and that I am loved and cherished regardless of any cage; then, the iron bars begin to disappear.

> I was neurotic for years. I was anxious and depressed and selfish. Everyone kept telling me to change. I resented them, and I agreed with them, and I wanted to change, but simply couldn't, no matter how hard I tried. Then one day someone said to me, "Don't change. I love you just as you are." Those words were music to my ears: "Don't change, Don't change. Don't change…I love you as you are." I relaxed. I came alive. And suddenly I changed!"—ANTHONY DE MELLO

To know that our cages—even the ones of iron and steel—are self-imposed, is a start. To recognize our capacity. And to live from sufficiency and strength and not limitation. Perhaps one of the biggest heartbreaks in our lives is that freedom is possible, yet we can pass our years trapped in the same old patterns. Entangled in some kind of trance — scripts about unworthiness or marginalization or shame or powerlessness or inadequacy — self-judgment and anxiety become the very cage. We spend our days in restlessness and dissatisfaction. And like Mohini, we grow incapable of accessing the freedom and peace that are our birthright.

I spent Saturday with a good group of folk at Mission San Luis Obispo de Tolosa, on California's central coast. We talked about finding and creating sanctuary. Places where we are replenished and nourished. And all the ways in a world of hurry and distraction that we can be derailed or stuck. And how, for whatever reason, we continue to believe whatever label is attached to the stuckness.

So where to begin? Maybe, all it takes is one step over the imaginary line of the cage in the corner.

"Our deepest fear is not that we are inadequate," Marianne Williamson reminds us. "Our deepest fear is that we are powerful beyond measure. It is our light, not our darkness that most frightens us. We ask ourselves, 'Who am I to be brilliant, gorgeous, talented, fabulous?' Actually, who are you not to be? You are a child of God. Your playing small does not serve the world. There is nothing enlightened about shrinking so that other people won't feel insecure around you. We are all meant to shine, as children do. We were born to make manifest the glory of God that is within us. It's not just in some of us; it's in everyone. And as we let our own light shine, we unconsciously give other people permission to do the same. As we are liberated from our own fear, our presence automatically liberates others."

Today, I choose to honor…

It is autumn here now. I love these October days, still filled with the last bit of sunshine and warmth, the garden basking and preening and aflame. I'm home tonight, and step outside to savor the evening sky. The moon is not bright, so the stars are endless and I remember that the sky's the limit, like my life...boundless and beckoning. I wonder if tomorrow I will be pacing in the corner or exploring the margins.

• • • • •

You never know where you'll learn lessons about sufficiency. For me, it happened sitting in a beauty salon chair, in underground Atlanta.

"Hi, I'm Sharon. You ready?" Her accent Southern.

I follow her. "Can you make me look young, distinguished, and handsome?" I ask.

She cocks her head, glances back and says, "Well...I can do young."

Whatever. I'm in Atlanta with a conference for Spiritual Directors International, doing a presentation about how spiritual care is grounded in self-care. I have a window of time and need a haircut. So I take the recommendation of the concierge and find myself in a salon near the hotel, following a young hairdresser toward a chair in the back of the salon.

One of my philosophies is this: In a barber chair—an inevitability on par with airplanes and bank teller lines—conversation is a bother. Just cut my hair and let me go. After all, I have important stuff to do.

Because she makes me laugh, I break my rule about staying mute saying that maybe a buzz cut is in order, telling Sharon about my father's decision after cancer to enjoy his new hair-free, carefree look.

"I'm a cancer survivor too," she says. "Just finished my chemo."

OK. I wasn't ready for that. Because if there is conversation, these chairs are for small talk only—no different than coffee hour after church.

"I'm sorry," I say. "When did you learn about the cancer, and what kind of treatment did you go through?"

"I had the whole nine yards," she laughs. "Surgery. And then more surgery and then chemo."

We are quiet, except for the sound of scissors. "It's the best thing that ever happened to me," she adds.

I've heard people say that—about tragedy or loss or heartbreak or misfortune—but am honestly unsure what to think. How can such a statement be true?

I do know that something inside us wants (needs) to find a silver lining, a way to make sense of what appears to be an utterly sense-less invasion of our body, or life, or world. I watch her in the mirror. Sharon is young, mid-thirties, petite, her facial features delicate and freckled, carrying a youthful innocence. There is no sign of any recent clash with the drug treatments that traumatize body and spirit, all in the name of health.

She looks into the mirror and holds my gaze. "It has made me softer," she tells me. "And now, I love different."

A single mother, Sharon talks about her fifteen-year-old daughter, in a tenor both wistful and filled with pride. She describes a young girl whose life was turned upside down with the possibility of a moth-er's death. And about a renewed relationship between mother and daughter. I nod. I understand.

"We never know," she continues. "A year ago if you had told me that this is where I'd be, I'd have told you you're crazy. But not now. Now I look at people different."

I compliment her hair. Quickly realizing my error, I try to apologize.

But Sharon shakes her head, tossing her hair, looking cute and sassy. "Thanks. I made it. It's something I do now. It's my calling. To make personal wigs for people going through chemo so they can look beau-tiful on the outside and feel beautiful on the inside."

Go figure. I'm at a conference with spiritual directors from different faith traditions around the world, and my moment of enlighten-ment and grace is gifted to me in a beauty-salon-barber-chair. I was taught—in church—as a boy, that we should love one another. You know, practice kindness and compassion.

Sufficiency is grounded on that core truth that, in Jesus's words, "You are the light of the world." You are, even in life's conundrums and softness, enough. Not only enough. But the soft heart allows you to be fully alive, fully engaged, to honor the gifts that may have been dormant, and that our heart brings to this world. But here's the deal: Love can only spill from a heart that has been softened and in most cases broken. In these encounters—if I do give or offer my heart—it does come back to me in better shape. Because it comes back to me, softer.

There is no doubt that when faced with tragedy or chaos or uncertainty or misfortune, we want to have a handle on it, or fix it, or make it go away. But this is not about a way to figure life out. Nor is it about determining whether we have intentionally or unintentionally invited chaos or sickness into our world. It's about the permission to see the world—this day—through the eyes of our heart. Our heart made soft.

It happens when…

> …we allow ourselves to feel, fully and wholly; without a need to defend, justify, or explain;
> …we allow ourselves to receive love and kindness without suspicion;
> …we are free to embrace a core of strength and courage that resides inside us; and let it spill to those around us;
> …we embrace sufficiency.

During his time with His Holiness the Dalai Lama, at his residence in exile in India in 2015, Archbishop Desmond Tutu wrote:

> In generosity, there is a wider perspective, in which we see our connection to all others. There is a humility that recognizes our place in the world and acknowledges that at another

time we could be the one in need, whether that need is material, emotional, or spiritual. There is a sense of humor and an ability to laugh at ourselves so that we do not take ourselves too seriously. There is an acceptance of life, in which we do not force life to be other than what it is. There is a forgiveness of others and a release of what otherwise might have been. There is a gratitude for all that we have been given. Finally, we see others with a deep compassion and a desire to help those who are in need.[15]

After the Atlanta conference someone asked me, "What did you do there?"

Well, I got a haircut. And I practiced the sacrament of the present. And I welcomed the power of sufficiency. And I felt my heart soften just a little.

Try This

Have you ever tried the verbal affirmation, "It is enough"?

After an ordinary moment…a sip of coffee / tea, watching the light slant through the window / trees, a pet on our lap, a smile from a friend / family, laughter, body ache after working in the garden, chocolate, watching children play, playing with children, fill in the blank…say, to yourself or even better, out loud, "It is enough".

Chapter Eleven

Embrace Epiphanies

We need to make room for surprise; take time to watch and observe;
and quit "doing" long enough to receive...Sabbath—rest, worship,
release—cleans out our inner houses, making room for God to
surprise us with wonder.—EUGENE PETERSON

I perform admiration. Come with me and do the same.
—MARY OLIVER

A woman stands at the window and stares. We are on the morning
commuter ferry from Vashon Island to Seattle. A snow-
covered Mount Rainier dominates the panorama. It stands
prominent, imperial in the dawn light. (It is true. Here in the
Northwest, the first time you see Mount Rainier, you do a double take.
Some divine sleight of hand. Where'd that mountain come from?)
The woman is wide-eyed, as if she is surprised by the mountain. As
if she is seeing it for the first time. All of the other early morning
commuters (and there are many) go about their business: Reading the
newspaper, drinking coffee, paying bills, talking with friends, napping
on benches.

"Looook," she announces loudly, "we can see the mountain.
Everybody looook!"

She has the demeanor of a person "not quite all there." You know
what I mean. She is clearly one of those people who embarrass us.
(Or realistically, one of those people we choose to ignore.) As other

commuters walk by, they (we) knowingly smile at one another and roll our eyes. She's not normal, we tell one another in code.

"Looook," she says again, pointing this time, almost reverential, "the mountain."

I've seen the mountain a thousand times, but I figure, "What the heck." So I put down my book, and look.

The rising sun has just crested the Cascade Mountain ridgeline. It looks as if it is sitting in a saddle between two peaks. The shaft of light from the sun glistens on the snow face of the Cascades, the color of a good English beer. It hits the Puget Sound and dances across the water, now a golden pathway from the ferry to the sky. Rainier, backlit and venerable in this morning light, appears etched, as if a great artist rendered it in charcoal or pen and ink. The water of the Puget Sound is gunmetal grey and calm. To the south is Tacoma harbor, where a crescent moon hangs in what I can only describe as a melancholy blue sky.

I do not pick up my book again.

I look. A morning vista as sacrament—a dose of grace; a brew, fortifying and settling.

"Looook," the woman is talking again. "The mountain. Everyone looook, the mountain."

To exit the ferry, we walk by the woman (still standing, still pointing, still talking), wondering, I suppose, what went wrong in her life, what finally snapped, and what made her leave her senses. How sad for her. We walk hurriedly, you know, in order to take care of those more important obligations awaiting us in our day.

On this morning, the "crazy woman" is my sage. My seer, my rabbi, my priest, my pastor. She is my reminder. For whatever reason, she sees the day without the extra layers of defense. (Or if you'll permit an impenitent play on words, she seizes the day, *carpe diem*.)

I tell this story whenever I can. And if you've heard me speak, chances are you've heard this story. And whenever I tell it, I get goose-flesh. This much is certain: Every time I tell it, I absorb the miracle… It's not just that the young woman looked. She embraced an epiphany.

An epiphany is an intuitive grasp of experience. As if a light bulb comes on, with an illumination, realization, or insight. Or simply, a moment when you get gooseflesh. The young woman embraced this moment, honoring it with her whole being. There is for her a very visceral engagement. She is, literally, all in. This is what I would love to bottle and sell…She didn't need permission. She didn't need approval. She didn't need skepticism. She didn't need a motivation to impress. She didn't need evaluation or justification. She needed simply this…"Looook how beautiful," she says, "the mountain."

Not long ago, I told the "Looook" story to a group of health care-givers in Washington State. Many were professionals. Others, care-givers not by choice, but encumbered with the daunting responsibility of caring for an ailing or dying loved one. (No, I can't yet imagine.) My assignment with the group? To talk about living a balanced life (I'll give you a hint—it's not possible). And, to talk about the reality of compassion fatigue and what it means to be a caregiver.

Before I talked, though, I needed to listen. "Tell me what you carry?" I asked the group gathered. "What weighs you down? What is the bunkum?" And they eagerly answered as I made a list of responses on a whiteboard.

"We feel invisible. We try and try and still can't fix it. We feel the guilt. We juggle grief. We feel unwanted. We learn to cope only to find the expectations keep changing. We can't find time for refueling." And the list went on.

What they didn't need from a guest speaker, was more advice heaped on their very full plates. What they needed was the permission to stop. The permission to breathe. The permission to looook.

Life is difficult. And sometimes, too heavy. We don't give ourselves the grace to feel exasperated or disheartened (you know, without guilt). And we don't give ourselves the grace to be seen or embraced. Because to receive grace, let alone wholeheartedly, is not an easy thing.

Here's my take on the story about the young woman at the ferry window: To see (life in its mysterious and extravagant fullness) begins with an inner disarmament. Sooner or later we need to remove pieces of the armor we wear that keeps us from allowing life in. Most of the time, I prefer the armor. My armor keeps me safe. But it also keeps me from seeing. From feeling. From paying attention. But, hey, it's a small price to pay. At least I'm not crazy.

It is no secret that we numb ourselves. And it's all too easy to point the finger at those whose drug comes in pill or needle form. Trouble is, I have found that distraction, if only, the need for perfection, resentment, fear, apathy, being a victim, and shame, are just as effective. They all serve the same purpose: censor. Each one numbing us, which keeps troublesome feelings (grief, sorrow, sadness, dejection, anger) at bay. But sadly, it does the same with epiphanies and wonder (ecstasy, awe, amazement, grace).

Public opinion is a powerful thing. I think about how we (on the ferry boat) conspired to agree about the crazy woman. "We're sane, she's crazy," we reassured each other with that knowing glance. Is it possible that we need numbers on our side, because deep down, we know that only "crazy" people can see? That the Spirit of God can madden us, and drive us, literally, out of our senses (or is it fully into our senses?).

Is that what I'm afraid of, intoxication with this life? What Rabbi Abraham Heschel called "radical amazement." What if we are here on this earth to get lost:

to fall in love with life;
to give in to the courage to be mad with the wonder of it all;
to live and dance on the edge of grace;
to dance with manatees;
to dance where we have nothing to show to justify our existence?

And the young woman's gift to herself? Gladness. The gladness—to just be. But here's the deal. This gladness doesn't tidy our life. It doesn't remove pain or sorrow or grief. It does however let us see the sacred in the midst. It does let us live smack dab in the middle of ordinary. It does let us embrace the sacrament of the present. It does let us live wholehearted, no matter what comes our way.

I didn't say that any of this is easy. Just that it is worth it. Borrowing from Barbara Brown Taylor, that which draws me to faith is not the believing parts, but the beholding parts. In other words, awe always precedes faith. Seeing allows awe. And awe gives birth to gratitude. Which means, in the words of Meister Eckhart, "If the only prayer you said in your whole life was, 'thank you,' that would suffice."

Today the weather couldn't decide; rain showers, and the clouds move on like swift set changes giving way to sunlight and optimism. I found the time to begin spring cleaning on a couple of garden beds, one with lavender blooms of Iris Reticulata peeking through the debris. The first spring flower in my garden. And a reminder that there is always hope. In this case, a hope regally attired.

● ● ● ● ●

Going through his five-year-old son's backpack, a father found a picture of a little boy standing under a rainbow crying. His first thought was, "Oh, God, my son is having some serious problems." When he asked his son about the picture, the little boy told his father that he had been playing at school and he saw a rainbow. "Dad," the little boy said, "the rainbow was so beautiful it made me cry."

The child is arrested by (captivated by, rapt in, awestruck by, absorbed in) beauty. Why? Because he has no restrictor plate in his soul.

> All of earth is crammed with heaven,
> and every bush aflame with God,
> but only those who see take off their shoes.
> —ELIZABETH BARRETT BROWNING

The child experiences his rainbow moment "without shoes." He embraces the epiphany.

I agree with Amy Rosenthal, "If rainbows did not exist and someone said wouldn't it be cool to paint enormous stripes of color across the sky, you'd say yes, 'That would be very cool—impossible but very cool.' Children are totally tuned into the miracle of rainbows—that's why they are forever drawing them."

In the world of a child, awe precedes faith. In our adult world, we place a premium on belief (or belief systems) instead of awe. We put the cart before the horse. Somewhere down the road our filter (as adults we have filters—which act like security checkpoints—for evaluating, judging and appraising events or emotions on a cost-benefit basis) removes us (distances us) from the experience:

> ...from our emotions,
> ...from our yearning,
> ...from our pain,
> ...from our prayers.

It reminds me of the woman who told me that her prayer time (a daily rosary) was always bogged down by the fear that she "wasn't doing it correctly."

"To pray is to take notice of the wonder," Rabbi Heschel writes, "to regain a sense of the mystery that animates all being, the divine margin in all attainment; prayer is our humble answer to the inconceivable surprise of living." Jesus is unequivocal. "Unless you change and become like little children, you will never enter the kingdom of heaven." For children, wonderment grows in the soil of surprise. Embracing epiphanies is all about our capacity to receive.

My friend tells me the story about an ecumenical and integrated church service, held in northern Louisiana. She attended the service with her priest. The service integrated black and white clergy of various denominations, including black Methodist and black Baptist preachers. It featured a choir from one of the local black Baptist churches.

For my friend, raised in Louisiana, having lived her life in a segregated world, this was a new and challenging experience. The service began, and she was wholly enthralled. She felt it, viscerally, the way the music lifted her up, nourishing and full of joy. It surrounded her, and filled the sanctuary. It was her first experience in a church where she "gave in" to being enraptured. Absorbing the music, inspired by the preaching, feeling a connection to the people around her—in pews filled with all manner of folk, mingled color and status, shared smiles and laughter—she told herself, "This is what heaven will be like." She let her tears flow freely.

In the car after, beginning the drive home, her priest said (in a tone undisguised), "Wasn't that positively dreadful?" He continued by listing all the problems and blunders with the liturgy, oblivious to the woman's joy. His words stung. She sat silent, assuming she had done something wrong to give in to such unadulterated joy.

Without wonder, or an ability to receive, our identity is defined by consumerism. In other words, value is now proffered on what is purchased or earned or produced. We equate our happiness with owning and consuming. So, it is not surprising that we are trained (acclimated) to see beauty in "high-end" merchandise.

We have moved from wonderment to consumption. It becomes the very antithesis of beauty, because it is predicated on rushing, hurry, and urgency. There is an attempt to "Christianize" it, by adding Jesus or God to the price tag. Eugene Peterson points out that in the end we have some kind of "spiritual self-help consumerism (lead, teach, garden and cook like Jesus; 3, 4, 5, 10, or 21 laws, steps, or plans for the meaningful life), all of which leave us busier, more accomplished, but never filled."

Sadly, we wean our children from wonder. I love the practice in Jewish tradition: children are given a taste of honey on their tongues during the celebration of the Torah. This is to remind them that the word of God is "sweet as honey" (Ezekiel 3:3).

The consumer myth tells me that there is something else I must add to my life. But savoring—embracing epiphanies—is not about addition. It is about subtraction. You see, I begin by removing the restrictor plate, and removing my shoes. When I do, I see that there is a connection between paying attention and savoring (mindfulness). Here's what I know: If I am rushing, I do not see. If I do not see, I am not present. If I am not present, I am not mindful and I cannot savor this moment.

On the seventh day, God rested. God savored. Savoring is rooted in Sabbath. For six days we work, we build, create, and control. The seventh day we rest. We stop. We receive. We savor. Without savoring, we assume reality is only about what we create or produce. If we honor (weigh heavy) embracing epiphanies, there are three outcomes:

One, we are free to live *this* life. Meaning that we are not driven to live another life, a different life, a down-the-road life. We find wonder here. As children, we find the kingdom of God, here. There is a scene in the movie *Shawshank Redemption* when Andy locks himself in the warden's office, puts a record on the turntable, and sets the prison intercom microphone near the speaker. The music pervades and suffuses the entire prison. Red, the narrator, says, "I have no idea to this day what those two Italian ladies were singing about. Truth is, I don't want to know. Some things are best left unsaid. I'd like to think they were singing about something so beautiful, it can't be expressed in words, and makes your heart ache because of it. I tell you, those voices soared higher and farther than anybody in a gray place dares to dream. It was like some beautiful bird flapped into our drab little cage and made those walls dissolve away, and for the briefest of moments, every last man in Shawshank felt free."

Two, we savor beauty and epiphanies and resurrection in places we don't expect. Another friend wrote, "I worked with my hands in the dirt, and it was saving me. The dirt was. How my hands felt digging. Gripping on the roots. The smells out there. The dark mornings. It made me feel stronger than I was. Because I had my hands on the earth. And the earth needed my hands or so it seemed. And for those hours I didn't think much, or if I did, the thoughts didn't feel as oppressive constrictive."

In the mud.

In the stranger in the pew.

In a child's rainbow drawing.

I love Meredith Hall's comment, "My mother craves the beauty of these storms. She teaches me to crave beauty—lonely, tumultuous, cleansing beauty."

Three, when I am present, I am grateful. And gratitude is always, always a type of prayer.

Again, I turn to Rabbi Heschel:

> We do not step out of the world when we pray; we merely see
> the world in a different setting. The self is not the hub, but the
> spoke of the revolving wheel. In prayer, we shift the center

of living from self-consciousness to self-surrender. God is the center toward which all forces tend. Prayer takes the mind out of the narrowness of self-interest, and enables us to see the world in the mirror of the holy. For when we betake ourselves to the extreme opposite of the ego, we can behold a situation from the aspect of God.

I never want to lose that childlike curiosity and artistry inside me. I'm home for a week or so, and the garden is abounding and teeming with life and color and enchantment. The peony buds profligate, the bearded iris blooms beguiling, the columbine exquisite. The branches of the Japanese maple, heavy with spring rain, deferentially bow. I once asked my analyst why I was in therapy. He told me it would make me a better gardener. Gardening can be strong medicine, an elixir that nurtures and shapes the soul. For that reason, it is a tonic seldom taken straight with no ice. Gardening has a way of seeping into your soul, and one day you find yourself, in the words of poet May Sarton, spending the first half hour of the morning "enjoying the air and watching for miracles," the joy and light still alive.

• • • • •

I re-watched *Fearless*, Jet Li's movie based on the true story of Huo Juanjia (1878–1910), the son of a great fighter (and teacher of Chinese martial arts) who refuses to teach Huo to fight. But Huo learns on his own, and wins. With each win, the taste of victory and pride comingle. He grows up fueled by an unquenchable anger, without any awareness why. Only that his solution to appease this compulsion is to continue to fight fueled by an eagerness to annihilate his opponents. His closest friend, Nong Jinsun, asks him, "When is enough? How many people do you need to defeat?"

Voracious isn't it? Can we ever truly get enough of what we don't need? (Doesn't take much to know it to be true, thinking of the dopamine of our day, our obsession with securing likes for a Facebook post.) A hunger for acknowledgment and a wounded pride make a lethal combination.

After Huo kills a rival (completely out of revenge, and with no remorse) over what turns out to be a false accusation, Huo's life unravels. A disciple of this rival takes his own revenge, killing Huo's mother and his young daughter. How does one stop any cycle of violence—whether it is to others or to ourselves?

Huo hits bottom, ashamed and filled with grief. The movie down-shifts, Huo spends time wandering, rescued by a grandmother and her blind granddaughter (Yueci, or "Moon"), and is nursed back to health, and nursed back to life, in their isolated village.

In one poignant scene, Huo is working in the fields planting rice. He is still fueled by a need to compete with his coworkers, still driven by a compulsion to finish first, and his work motions are manic. The wind freshens, a breeze blows, and the tree leaves rustle. His coworkers (in fact, all the workers in the entire village) stop what they are doing. They stop. They stand. They close their eyes. They feel the breeze on their faces. They inhale. They find refreshment. They find epiphanies in the very, very ordinary. And for this moment, it is enough.

Huo looks at the workers' behavior, puzzled. His pace, his require-ment to win or profit at all costs blinds him to both his need and the remedy. (Like the German story about the man chopping wood with a blunt ax. He works exhausted, too tired to stop even in order to sharpen his ax.) It is enough. The sentence rolls so easily off the tongue. And yet...

There is a scene where Huo's friend Nong attempts to dissuade him from this path of revenge. But to no avail. How easy it is to be blind.

I shouldn't be surprised because I know firsthand what it is like to blindly play out a script (written by Lord knows whom!). To go through the motions, as if our identity is imprisoned or constricted by this false or hungry self. And like Huo, we still haven't found what we're looking for. Pain (physical, emotional, spiritual) hijacks our world (to the point that there are days when we don't even know what to Google). We lose our way. And often we don't know why. Except, we tell ourselves, this doesn't feel right. And we set about trying to remedy it. However, you can't fix anything using the same thinking that got you in trouble in the first place.

So when our wounds speak, why must we assume they are the whole story? Jean Vanier (founder of L'Arche) invites us to take a different path, "Look at your own poverty, welcome it, cherish it, don't be afraid. Share your death because thus you will share your love and your life."

I have a friend who has been living for some time with real pain; end-of-life pain. And yet, in her conversation she speaks of living with a deep sense of peace.

Deep peace? Yes. That's exactly what I wish for. It is exactly what Huo clamored for. So, there must be a trick, right? Or, perhaps, like the villagers…

> We stop.
> We stand.
> We close our eyes.
> We feel the breeze on our faces.
> We inhale.
> We find refreshment.
> And for this moment, it is enough.

Yes, epiphanies, even here. In the very ordinary of every day.

Peace comes when we see the difference between doing battle with life's obstacles, adversities, and bleakness, and seeing this battle as an uninterrupted and debilitating struggle. As if every day is an ongoing antagonism that leaches the life and spirit out of us. Yes, life is difficult.

Yes, obstacles are weighty and real. But if we see obstacles only as a struggle, our mindset has capitulated to the next bigger and badder thing. And we never arrive, do we?

This is important: We are not being asked to let go of the obstacle. But we can let go of the struggle. In an odd way, our letting go is predicated on a holding onto. Meaning that this obstacle—whether it be pain or fear or limitation—is wrapped around an incredible and grace-filled gift. That gift is *this* sacred moment. And when we stop, we can find it, see it, and embrace it. When we stop we let go of fear, because this moment is enough. When we stop we can fall back into outstretched arms. The name is not as important as trusting that the arms are there.

The good news? We find deep peace and resolve in our own skin, because there is nothing left to prove. It is enough just to be Terry. For this moment, it is enough.

Today, I am riding the ferry from Seattle, on my way back to the island. Our winter ceiling has lifted today, and the entire region is bathed in sunshine. Now, at dusk, the cloud cover is scattered, like tattered pieces of cloth. Beyond the Olympic Mountains to the west, the sky is spring blue, baby-boy blue. The Puget Sound water is ice blue. And the mountains are blanketed with snow. In the clear winter air, the mountains stand stalwart: enduring, comforting and settling. They are bigger than any of my pettiness. And their beauty slows my breathing and eases my mind. I had planned to write more about beauty, but the mountains enlighten me…

It is enough, just to sit, just to savor.

Try This

Take a walk. The distance doesn't have to be far nor the walk strenuous. Choose a destination (two to five minutes away)—around the block, to the end of the street, through a park, around your garden. I want you to walk to that destination as quickly as possible, thinking only about the destination, as if you had on blinders. When you arrive, pause. Literally. For at least two or three minutes. Breathe.

Now, return using the exact same route, only this time I want you to take at least twenty minutes on the return. You can dawdle, meander or mosey, your choice.

What do you see that you missed the first time?

What do you hear or smell or notice?

Everything that is newly noticed is an epiphany.

Chapter Twelve

Live Undefended; Live without Fear

God calls you to be. —FREDERICK BUECHNER

If you're wearing a disguise for too long, it will be difficult for the mirror to recognize you. At the end of the day I hope you become the person they didn't expect you to be. Be proud to wear you.
—DODINSKI

At any given moment, we have the power to say: This is not how the story is going to end.

Mr. Rogers stepped out of a Manhattan subway train onto the platform. A group of people recognized him, including a young mother with her six-year-old son. The boy brandished a Star Wars lightsaber, and was intent on whacking everything—and everyone—in his path. This included Mr. Rogers.

The mother stood mortified, "Honey, please don't hit Mr. Rogers! I think it's illegal. And it's not polite."

Oblivious (and doing what Mr. Rogers does best, which is to "ignore" the adult and talk with the child), Fred Rogers drops to his knees, next to the boy, now eye to eye. He whispers to the boy. The boy whispers back and puts away his lightsaber. Goodbyes were exchanged.

One hour later, the people traveling with Mr. Rogers had enough suspense. "You have got to tell us what you said to the boy!"

Mr. Rogers smiled, "I told him, 'We are a lot alike. I have a sword too. Not as nice as yours. Mine is wood. I keep it inside me, for all the times I don't feel strong. When I think I need to impress people, I take my sword out, and I believe that when people see the sword they will think I'm strong. But when I feel strong inside, I know I don't need my sword, and I put it away. Looking in your eyes right now, I know you are a loved little boy, and I see you are very strong on the inside. The little boy said, 'I guess I don't need my sword today.'"[16]

I never get tired of reading about Mr. Rogers. I miss him. And I love this story because that little boy is me. I know what it is like to not feel strong on the inside. I know what it is like to take out my sword, and do my best to impress everyone around me. I know what it is like to take out my sword in order to appear stronger than I feel. I also know that life's pace (and the stuff that gets in the way) exacerbates the conundrum. As if we assume that our identity is predicated on the sum of consumption and distraction (more) plus velocity (hurry). And our mantra becomes, "This is not enough." (Meaning this relationship or job or circumstance or new toy or prayer or faith or conversation or moment, or whatever.) And as a result, I am (we are) not present. And given my need to impress—or consume or use or add or rush—I end up whacking everything around me with my sword. Just a hint: that never seems to work out so good. And that is when my life too easily becomes "garbled."

I write this during a week of another mass shooting, which has been unnerving for all of us in the United States. A week where we are all hurting. And grieving. We have witnessed scenes of violence we cannot understand or comprehend. And a knee-jerk toward unhelpful and inflammatory rhetoric on both sides. As if we need to whack somebody. In all of that, there are swords. And here's how living from fear affects me day to day. I am afraid to live with my heart unclenched and expanded. I can too easily walk as a resentment in search of a cause. And that's why I needed Mr. Rogers today: "Terry, you can put away your sword."

Because here's the deal: It doesn't matter what we expect from life, but what life expects from us. As a result, we can choose to unleash the heart, choose to honor living undefended, in order to be our better selves. And no one can take that away. They can demean us, belittle us, criticize us, and silence us. But no one can take that capacity away. I needed Mr. Rogers's reminder that there is a word spoken about me. It tells me that I am strong on the inside. And not because of anything I have done or failed to do.

I confess that I take some perverse pride in knowing that I've used my sword skillfully at times in my life. That must count for something. I do know that my need for a sword reinforces two things.

First: We live in a world that worships power. Or at the very least, we are in awe of it. We "know" that the strong and powerful and muscular win. The strong come out on top. Questioning such a paradigm is precisely what made Jesus so unnerving. He turned the paradigm on its head. "Wait a minute. You're a Messiah (strong and influential and formidable, a hero) and yet you let yourself be crucified?"

Questioning such a paradigm is precisely what made St. Francis so unnerving. He too, turned the paradigm on its head. When he says no to the trappings of power and entitlement, he chooses, quite publically, to put his sword away. He chooses instead to live from the sufficiency that is already within, not needing to find meaning or influence or power from whatever (on the outside) is added to his life.

Second. If I don't pay attention to the wound that is threatened, I give way to an impulsive and careless reaction, and am now at the mercy of that reaction. The reaction owns me, whether it be anxiety or anger or resentment, or even violence.

Today, I will put my sword down...

Today, I will honor...

• • • • •

For twenty-five years in Invercargill, at the south end of New Zealand, Burt Munro works on increasing the speed of his motorcycle, a 1920 Indian Scout. He dreams of taking his Indian Scout to the Bonneville Salt Flats to see how fast it can go. By the early 1960s, heart disease threatens his life, so he mortgages his house and takes a boat to Los Angeles, buys an old car, builds a makeshift trailer, gets the Indian through customs, and heads for Utah. Along the way, people he meets are charmed by his open, direct friendliness. The uncertainty is still real. If he makes it to Bonneville, will they let an old coot race on the flats, with makeshift tires, no brakes, and no chute?

And yes, they did. In 1967, Burt set the land-speed world record.

Before his trip, his young neighbor Tom (maybe aged twelve) asks him why he's going to all the trouble.

"I'll live more in five minutes on that bike than some people live in a lifetime. And if you don't follow through on your dream you might as well be a vegetable."

"What kind of vegetable?" Tom asks.

"A cabbage," Burt tells the boy.[17]

Well, I don't want to be a cabbage, so let the spiritual adventure begin.

Today, I will choose to honor…

OK, so maybe we don't become a cabbage, but we do find ways to give up who we are—the reservoir inside of us, filled with hopes, dreams, generosity, and yearnings—for who we think we should be. Perhaps because we think our lives will be safer and less troubled? I don't know when that coaxing toward precaution started for you. I do know that whatever was censored—however long ago—is still inside, alive and well. Live with regret if you wish, but it will only compound what is already lost.

The alternative? In the words of poet Mary Oliver, "Tell me, what is it you plan to do with your one wild and precious life?"

Whenever I get a dose of Mary Oliver "music," it does my spirit good.

> I tell you this
> to break your heart,
> by which I mean only
> that it break open and never close again
> to the rest of the world.
> —MARY OLIVER

Yes. And Amen.

Living from an open heart (our swords put away) always takes us beyond our ego. We do not need to live defensive. And do you know what spills from an open heart? Generosity, benevolence, empathy, gladness, gratefulness, compassion and kindness. Here's a word of caution: We do not honor living undefended as if there's some club to join, complete with secret instruction manual and stealthy handshake. As if there is something else we need to add to our lives to make it successful, or meaningful, or palatable, or boost our self-esteem. To honor is much more fundamental.

So, we begin with this question: Today, am I willing to be loved for being this me?

If the answer is yes, then I guess I don't need my sword today. If the answer is yes, I can unleash my heart, and hear the good news about my better self. If the answer is yes, then the choices I make will spill to the people and world around me. There's the power. This spilling ("this little light of mine") invites grace into the world around us.

I heard Brian McClaren talk about the Genesis creation story. Genesis says that God created and called it good. Notice this: God did not call it perfect. Meaning what? Meaning that if it were perfect, we would merely be a maintenance crew. Instead, we are very active co-creators, involved in the process...the ongoing and unfolding of

God's presence in this world. Yes. As co-creators we are invited to approach life with open arms. To live vulnerable. Or, in the words of Alan Jones, "I want to know if joy, curiosity, struggle, and compassion bubble up in a person's life. I'm interested in being fully alive."

And I say, Amen.

So, tell me, where does joy, curiosity, struggle, and compassion bubble up in your life? Because that bubbling up makes a difference. We are active co-creators. We can create bridges, knowing that swords disconnect us and we forget that no one of us is on this faith journey alone. We can create bridges for reconciliation and second chances and peacemaking. We can create roads for mercy and generosity and justice. We can create floors for dancing and music and celebration. We create bandages for wounds and fractured spirits and broken hearts. We create sanctuaries for safety and prayer and hope.

Tonight, I'm on the patio. At the birdfeeders a dozen or so vying for the good seats. I walk the garden. It grounds me. It is not long before dusk. In bloom, fire-red Crocosmia Lucifer, which never fails to make me smile. The air is cool, perfect to raise a glass, savor the moment. I sit on the patio until past dark. I wait for the stars. I put down my sword.

Try This

"This is one of our fears of quiet; if we stop and listen, we will hear this emptiness.... But this emptiness has nothing at all to do with our value or our worth. All life has emptiness at its core; it is the quiet hollow reed through which the wind of God blows and makes the music that is our life. Without that emptiness, we are clogged and unable to give birth to music, love, and kindness." —WAYNE MULLER

Be quiet long enough to hear the music God makes in your life. It will probably take some practice, but it will be worth the time you invest in it.

Chapter Thirteen

Relish the Sacred in the Ordinary

What is required to make a place holy?
The ordinary becoming extraordinary,
The common interrupted for a moment
that we wish would last forever,
God coming into our forest, decorating our trees,
Inviting us to remove our shoes.
—REV. ROBIN RINGLAND

Not knowing when the dawn will come,
I open every door.—EMILY DICKINSON

Christ learned about his mission while he was cutting wood and making chairs, beds, and cabinets. He came as a carpenter to show us that—no matter what we do—everything can lead us to the experience of God's love.—PAULO COELHO

My friend Tim Hansel was writing a book on parenting. So, he asked his young sons, "Boys, how do you know Dad loves you?"

He figured that they would say, "Daaaad, remember when you took us to Disney World, like for ten days!" They didn't say that, so he knew he wasted all that money.

He figured they'd say, "Daaaad, remember Christmas and you bought us all that great stuff!"

They didn't say that.

They said, "Dad, we know you love us, when you wrestle with us."

He remembered two times. He had come home, hungry, tired, late, and he didn't care. But these urchins were yanking on his pant leg. "So I rolled with them on the floor. Toward the kitchen," he said, "just to get them out of my way." And then it hit him. In the middle of that very ordinary, boring, mundane experience, real life was happening. Unfeigned joy, love, intimacy, connection, grace, sacrament—the really, really good stuff—all woven into the commonplace.

"But," Tim laments, "I missed it. Because I was only tuned into Disney World and Christmas."

There is nothing wrong with Disney World or Christmas. But they have meaning only because of the sacred in the ordinary. Because of the wrestling times. In our world, the word *ordinary* is a pejorative. "That was ordinary, I'll give that one star," we say, as if every encounter or vista or meal or conversation or experience or prayer requires a grade or review. As such, our mind has prejudged, already deciding to go into the moment armed with a label. Let's not forget that there's one big drawback: When we label anything, we dismiss it. And we are unable to receive. We are unable to savor. We are unable to relish.

So, what if ordinary walks and wrestling times are really our own road to Emmaus? Those ordinary places where our eyes are opened to see what we have missed and our heart burns within us. Someone asked me about New Year's resolutions. They were still equivocating and wondered what great plans I had made. Well, I had just come off a truly bad week, and wondered out loud what it means when the first few weeks of your new year don't go as planned. Do you get a do-over when it comes to resolutions? Or is the rest of your year downhill? Let's just say that the look on their face told me that they had hoped for a more cheerful response.

This reinforces to me how easy it is to buy into the myth that ordinary life proceeds according to our specifications and designs. My ability to handle disarray, disappointment, or chaos makes me wonder if it is that different from the questions I used to ask my son: "Have you had enough sleep? Have you had too much sugar?"

Or, in my case, at this moment, am I bonding with the incompetent idiot at the customer service counter? (Oops. That slipped out inadvertently.) So, in the airport—while writing this chapter about relishing the sacred—I was looking for that room where I could stew in the invigorating juices of exasperation and irascibility.

There is this hope—scarcely disguised—that each new year offers a cleansing. As if we wipe the slate clean of last year's tumult or disorder or blunders. I get it. I do. We want to eliminate worry. But it doesn't help if we see our freedom from interruption as linked to luck or goodness or faith. That's just another variation of closure. Or control.

Where was I? Oh yes, standing in the airport stewing. Thankfully, Bruce saved my emotional bacon. With my earbuds in, I cranked up Springsteen's "This Little Light of Mine." And though I didn't know how my day was going to end, I realized (stewing in a departure lounge) that this day, this moment, is still worth relishing.

St. Francis reminded us, in the way he lived and in the way he taught, that God is so very real in small gifts and simple pleasures. God is present in the commonplace, the weak, the flawed, the compromised. The profane is not the antithesis of the sacred, but the bearer of it. And that the light spills even from the profane. "I have been all things unholy," Francis wrote. "If God can work through me, he can work through anyone."

We are so bent on removing ourselves from the mundane (and certainly, the profane) that we miss miracles. And it is not surprising that once we see any sacred moment or miracle, we do our best to turn it into a project: Five Steps to Organize Wrestling Times. It is not easy for us to rest in the solace that God is present (in this very ordinary moment), having nothing to do with our faith or our effort to invest the moment with meaning. In other words, there is freedom in this gift of wrestling times.

> I don't need to craft the moment, I can live it.
>
> I don't need to read into the moment, I can receive it.
>
> I don't need to find control over the moment, I can let it be.
>
> I don't need to orchestrate closure in the moment, I can pay it forward.

When the Shawnee and Chippewa (and other early peoples) went on hunts or vision quests or long journeys, each traveler would carry in a small rawhide pouch various tokens of spiritual power—perhaps a feather, a bit of fur, a claw, a carved root, a pinch of tobacco, a pebble or a shell. These were not simple magical charms; they were reminders of the energies that sustain all of life. By gathering these talismans into a medicine pouch, the hunter, traveler, or vision seeker was recollecting the sources of healing and bounty and beauty.[18]

Their pouch, a way of declaring, "Today, I honor…" I like the image. And if wouldn't hurt us if we carried a medicine pouch. Or at least asked, What am I carrying with me today?

Knowing that these elements of the ordinary nourish and heal and sustain…offering hope, a will to live, wonder, fortitude, and a generosity of spirit.

Wrestling time…let's call it a whiff of the holy in the muddle of ordinary life. Can we see the gift there?

Back to Bruce and "This Little Light of Mine," it reminds me that…

> My light can shine even when I don't have all the answers.
>
> My light can shine even when everything doesn't add up.
>
> My light can shine even when the pieces of the puzzle don't make any sense.

Dad, we know you love us when you wrestle with us. Yes. This little light…there are gifts in the ordinary, the boring, and the mundane… gifts to embrace, gifts to receive and gifts to give.

• • • • •

My mind was given to football today. I had my lucky beer and lucky snacks and did my best to keep my heart from cardiac arrest. It turns out I needed more than one lucky beer. (Football fans will understand.) After the game, I sat in the living room. The game was, shall we say, nerve-racking. I was hypnotized by the flames in the fireplace and waited for my pulse to return to normal. I stepped outside to look up at the moon. It is resting, as if sitting on an upper branch of a large fir tree, and the entire garden poses, like an old-fashioned photo in sepia tone. I smile. Glad to relish the sacred in the ordinary.

Try This

In your journal reflect on this affirmation: When I pause, I put myself in a "new or different" environment. When I pause, I trigger those parts of my soul…the space to savor, relish, value, honor, share, welcome, invite, see, touch, celebrate, wonder, feel, to experience grace…. When I pause, I create spaces—or sanctuaries—in which renewal can be born. (For me it's a good exercise to practice using one of those verbs–savor or relish or celebrate for example–in naming out loud or in my mind what I am seeing…that this moment is real. And good for my soul…)

Chapter Fourteen

Walk One Another Home

We're all just walking each other home. —RAM DASS

Let someone love you just the way you are—as flawed as you might be, as unattractive as you sometimes feel, and as unaccomplished as you think you are. To believe that you must hide all the parts of you that are broken, out of fear that someone else is incapable of loving what is less than perfect, is to believe that sunlight is incapable of entering a broken window and illuminating a dark room. —MARC HACK

The ache for home lives in all of us. The safe place where we can go as we are and not be questioned. —MAYA ANGELOU

On a beach near the ocean, two very young children spend their afternoon enthusiastically building a sand castle. They work eager, unabashed, and wholehearted. Giggles and laughter fill the air. After they finish, they admire their handiwork. Focused, they do not notice the rising tide. In an instant, a wave flattens their castle. Joy drains from their faces, tears run freely, and delight turns to disbelief and sadness. All their effort. Gone.

If we had been watching, we would certainly feel their pain and wonder, no doubt, how they would handle the disappointment. Surely, their day is over. To the surprise of one bystander, after a few minutes of tears and distress, the children grab one another's hand and run up the beach, where they begin to build another sand castle.

We all have high tides, and waves that take out sand castles in our lives (be it dreams or plans or expectations or even hope). Watching the children run up the beach, it occurs to the bystander that the people who do make it (the people who endure and carry on) are those with a hand to hold. The children found solace, renewal, and confidence in the sanctuary of connection—a place where they knew they were safe. And embraced. And the sacrament of the present comes alive in that sanctuary.

Life happens. Sand castles flatten. And there's a part of me that needs to make sense of it all. I am certain that I would still be sitting in the sand near what used to be, shouting to the sky, "How could this happen…to me?!?" Before I can move on, I want to make sense of the waves and my rotten luck. Of course, the result isn't exactly what I had in mind. Instead of clarity, I become sad. Cautious. Afraid. Stuck. As long as I see only the misfortune and inconvenience, the flattened sand castle defines me. So, I buy this label, this new version of reality.

The good news? The children in this story were not undone by scarcity (or depletion or sadness). They went about their day as if sufficiency were their reality. And because it was their paradigm, in their vulnerability and awkwardness, they built a new sand castle.

I love this story. And whatever that is, I want it. OK, maybe it's not a new sand castle. But it is a new moment, a gift, a beacon of hope. Telling us that even in our vulnerability and awkwardness, we have the sufficiency to (we have the capacity to, we are wired to) risk, try, give, care, contribute, stand up, hold a hand, build another sand castle. Life is precarious, and sometimes it is more than just sand castles that are flattened. We live in a world where bombs are real.

Sadly, they feel too common. In April 2015, a car packed with explosives detonated in the busy Mansour district of Baghdad, killing at least ten people and injuring twenty-seven. After this incident, something very unusual happened. Karim Wasfi went to the bomb site, took out his cello, sat down on a chair amid ash and rubble in a black suit, his long hair combed back, and started to play. Why go to the site of a car bomb to play your cello?

Wasfi, the renowned conductor of the Iraqi National Symphony Orchestra, said simply, "The other side chose to turn every element, every aspect of life into a battle and into a war zone. I chose to turn every corner of Iraq into a spot for civility, beauty, and compassion. I wanted to show what beauty can be in the ugly face of car bombs, and to respect the souls of the fallen ones."[19]

We know that when he played, soldiers cried. People kissed. They clapped, they felt alive, they felt human, and they felt appreciated and respected. This does not surprise me. When I watched, I cried too. Because it touched something deep inside me. An invitation to live wholehearted in a broken world. And the power of having a hand to hold. No one is on this journey alone.

Let us walk one another home.

• • • • •

In chapter twelve, we talked about swords, and living defended. The act of putting down our sword allows our vulnerability to breathe. And Brené Brown reminds us that vulnerability is what makes us beautiful. And allows us to see the beauty in the world around us. So, without scotoma (selective blindness) our focus changes. We no longer see only what will hurt or injure or threaten. We now see ways that empathy and kindness and generosity give us greater access to the present moment, a place fueled by empathy and not suspicion.

As a storeowner tacked a sign above his door, "Puppies for Sale," a little boy appeared and asked. "How much are you going to sell those puppies for?"

The store owner replied "$50 each."

The little boy reached into his pocket and pulled out some change. "I have $2.37, can I have a look at them?"

The store owner smiled and whistled. Out of a kennel came Lady, followed by her five balls of four-legged fur. One puppy limped and lagged considerably. "What's wrong with that little dog?" the boy asked.

The store owner explained that the puppy was born without a hip socket, and the vet told him that the puppy would limp for the rest of its life. The little boy's face lit, "That's the puppy I want to buy!"

The store owner replied, "No, you don't. If you really want him, I'll give him to you."

The little boy did not hide his annoyance. "I don't want you to give him to me. He's worth every penny. I would like to give you $2.37 now, and 50 cents every month until he's paid for."

Taken aback, the store owner minced no words, "Young man, this puppy is never going to be able to run, jump, or play like other puppies!"

The boy reached down and rolled up his pant leg, to reveal a badly twisted, crippled left leg supported by a bulky metal brace. He looked up at the store owner, "Well, I don't run so well myself, and the little puppy will need someone who understands."

In *Brendan* (Frederick Buechner's novel about a sixteenth-century Irish saint), a servant recounts a conversation between Brendan and Gildas, a crippled and bitter old priest.

> "I am as crippled as the dark world," Gildas says.
>
> "If it comes to that, which one of us isn't my dear?" Brendan replies.
>
> Gildas with but one leg. Brendan sure he's misspent his whole life entirely. I who had left my wife to follow him and buried our only boy. The truth of what Brendan said stopped all our mouths. We was cripples all of us…

"To lend each other a hand when we're falling," Brendan
said, "Perhaps that's the only work that matters in the end."

We all see "crippled" parts of ourselves that sadden, discourage, infu-
riate, embarrass, or even repulse us. We know they are there. And
we see bunkum; some is our own making. Most not. Even so, we do
our best to wish or will or pray them away. It is not surprising that
we project this disdain for disease onto others. In the same way that
young St. Francis felt a disdain for lepers and avoided them at all
costs, our willful blindness sees only the "crippled" part and labels it
unspeakable.

In his *Testament*, Francis writes, "When I was in sin, the sight of
lepers nauseated me beyond measure; but then God himself led me
into their company, and I had pity on them. When I had once become
acquainted with them, what had previously nauseated me became a
source of physical consolation for me."

Francis soon found himself living with lepers and caring for them.
Or, in Richard Rohr's reminder, "The Lord comes to us disguised as
ourselves."

Our prayers are fueled by a world that sees imperfection as an indictment. And we pass judgment on our value, based upon that measure-
ment: appearance, achievement, and affluence. If only...If only...we
tell ourselves. Maybe it's about our illusion of control. With all our
fixing and renovating, look what we have to show for ourselves! "You
can have the life you DESERVE to live," an ad for a local plastic
surgeon promises. I have nothing against whiter teeth or a tighter back-
side. However, I'm not so sure that will take care of what troubles me.

The problem is this: As long as I am bent on fixing, repairing and
renovating in order to make myself more presentable or lovable or
acceptable, I am postponing the ability to receive any gifts (from you
or from God) in *this* present moment. One young volunteer, working

at L'Arche, Jean Vanier's homes for seriously handicapped adults, wrote of the residents, "They never ask what degree do you have, what university did you attend. They only ask, 'Do you love me?' In the end, isn't that what matters?"

Indeed. Here's the truth: We have the ability to receive, to be loved, to know our value, only from a place of vulnerability. Because in our nakedness, our "crippledness," our brokenness, and our vulnerability we have no power, no leverage, nothing to bargain with. Our identity is not dependent upon becoming somebody, impressing somebody, or removing all imperfection. We can be, literally, BE, at home in our own skin, damaged hip socket and all.

I was raised in a church that used the Scripture, "Be ye perfect as God is perfect," as a hammer meant to beat all the blemishes out of me. But here's the deal: Wholeness is not perfection. Wholeness is embodying—living into—this moment, be it happy or sad, full or empty, running or limping. Granted, there are flawed and weak parts that could change. But we can't change anything until we can love it. We can't love anything until we can know it. We can't know anything until we can embrace it.

And we touch wholeness at that place of vulnerability. In this place, we are human. In this place, we are sons and daughters of God. In this place, we hear God speak our name. The very image of God is imbedded in this fragile nature, in its very breakability. It is in that vulnerability where we find exquisite beauty—compassion, tender-heartedness, mercy, forgiveness, gentleness, openness, kindness, empathy, listening, understanding and hospitality. The alternative? To protect ourselves from all manner of breakability (and "crippledness") and to seal off our hearts and souls with Teflon. It is true; there will be no pain or brokenness. And, there will be no love.

I love what I do: talking, teaching, entertaining. But, if I'm honest, there are times when I wonder why I still do "what" I do. While it may not have been answered today, it made a difference when a man approached me to say, "Thank you. For the last few years, I've been floundering. This weekend you gave me permission to embrace who I am, and where I am." We touch wholeness at that place of vulnerability. I think we forget that it doesn't take much to be present. And to make a difference.

I love this scene from Fredrik Backman's *And Every Morning the Way Home Gets Longer and Longer* (a conversation between Noah and his grandpa):

> We have to write essays all the time! The teacher wanted us to write what we thought the meaning of life was once.
> "What did you write?"
> "Company."
> Grandpa closes his eyes.
> "That's the best answer I've heard."
> "My teacher said I had to write a longer answer."
> "So what did you do?"
> "I wrote: Company. And ice cream."
> Grandpa spends a moment or two thinking that over. Then he asks:
> "What kind of ice cream?"
> Noah smiles. It's nice to be understood.

As the old man walks the beach at dawn, he notices a young man picking up starfish and flinging them into the sea. Catching up to the youth, he asks a simple question, "Why are you doing this?"

The boy answers that the stranded starfish would die if left until the morning sun.

"But the beach goes on for miles, and there are millions of starfish. How can your efforts make any difference?"

The young man looked at the starfish in his hand and threw it to safety—into the ocean past the breaking waves. "It makes a difference to this one," he said.

Each new year brings its own push and pull, and a resolve to improve, or at the very least, give the impression that we are trying. Here in the Pacific Northwest, we've been blessed with a few dry days—blessed because it has been preceded by thirty consecutive rain days. When the sun splits the cloud cover, the vistas are arresting. Snow-covered Cascade and Olympic Mountain ranges, dazzling against the gunmetal-grey water of the Puget Sound.

As I write this, birds are at my feeder outside the window—our winter gang (the true snowbirds already sipping exotic drinks in their warmer environs) including black-capped chickadee, dark-eyed junco, nuthatch and titmouse. They rummage and dart and chirrup, and are not in the least preoccupied with tomorrow, or even the new year for that matter.

My heartbeat slows, and I put down my pen.

Try This

Let yourself be quiet for about a minute or so. It's time for a Gratitude Moment.

We are here, because of the gifts and presence of many people. Some in small ways, some in big ways. People who remind us that we are not on this journey alone. Bring those people to mind. What gift(s) did they give you by their presence in your life and world? If that person is still alive, today is a good day to say, "Thank You." Now, think of people where you can give a gift by your presence, even in a very small and ordinary way.

I was
looking for that shop
where the shopkeeper would say,
"There is nothing of value in here."
I found it and did not leave.
The richness of not wanting
wrote these poems.
—KABIR

A synagogue needed help. They were in dire straits, and morale was low. They called a famous rabbi to help them sort it out, to offer them insights and give them all the answers to the questions they were asking. On the evening the rabbi visited the synagogue, every pew was full, the congregation rapt, eager for wisdom and anticipated resolution.

As the rabbi stood silent, the audience squirmed, puzzled and a little unnerved. Then the rabbi began to sing, and to dance, glad hearted and effervescent. The music filled the church and the dancing rabbi made his way up the aisle, where he invited parishioners to join him. It wasn't long before every member of the congregation was dancing and the church walls reverberated with the spirit of the dance. All evening they danced.

After, they sat, still intoxicated with the joy of dancing. And only then did the rabbi speak, "I hope that I have provided all the answers to the questions you were asking."

Before we seek to manage life, it wouldn't hurt to just live it.

Before we seek to analyze life, it wouldn't hurt to just embrace it.

Before we seek to control life—nice and neat and tidy—it wouldn't hurt to just dance.

Which all sounds good on paper, until you realize that you've finished the dance, and still have no "answers."

With care the surgeon reiterates the essentials about the heart surgery to his patient, as the gurney is about to be rolled into the operating room. Regardless of how many times the surgeon has performed this procedure, he is aware that for each patient the anxiety is first-hand and not easily quelled. The patient's mind feels thick (perhaps the drugs), and while the words are understandable, the meaning is muddled. Seeing the patient's fear, the surgeon takes a model heart from a nearby shelf, shows it to the patient and says, "You brought me your heart. I'm going to give you back your heart. And it will be in better shape than the way you brought it to me."

Not a bad mantra for all human encounters. After all, we are hearts that touch. Which may sound too sentimental in a real world; where hearts touch and hearts hurt, hearts hope and hearts break, hearts heal and hearts splinter, and from those splintered places hearts give again and again. There's a part of us that wishes for a world where there are no broken hearts, but if that were the case, we'd miss all the good stuff.

There's a story about a magazine ad sponsored by the Humane Society, looking for homes for homeless pets. A photo of a puppy and kitten—looking up at you from the page—catches your eye and your heart. But it's the affirmation on the top of the ad that sticks, "It's who owns them that makes them important."

Part of the conundrum is that we see any upheaval or disorder or disenchantment as an indictment. Why? Because we live in a world where we are owned by the need for perfection or arrival or tidiness or answers (including the right creed). It is no wonder we so easily get derailed. It's a mentality summed up in this sermon excerpt; a cleric (apparently speaking for sectarians universal) forewarned the congregation, "Everyone is created by God, but not everyone is a child of God!"

He couldn't be more wrong. And as long as there is a voice in us that trumpets this message of scarcity and deficiency, we miss the invitation of the rabbi: Inside of every one of us—whether broken or splintered or lost or disoriented—is sufficiency, the exquisite beauty of a dancer and the child of God.

I wish I could show you, when you are lonely or in darkness, the astonishing light of your own being. —Hafiz

Recently I've had a few friends talk to me about crossroads in life. I used to pride myself in knowing what to tell people. But these conversations only served to remind me that the older I get, the more clueless I become, especially about relationships. But that's not necessarily a bad thing. Rainer Maria Rilke (in *Letters to a Young Poet*) writes to a young man: "Be patient toward all that is unsolved in your heart. And try to love the questions themselves. Do not seek the answers that cannot be given you because you would not be able to live them. And the point is to live everything. Live the questions now." Or, as the rabbi would say it, "Dance the questions now." And I would add, it's more fun to dance the questions with the manatees.

Today I was a guest preacher at the Vashon Lutheran Church. My second time in as many months. I wondered aloud if they were hoping the second time to be the charm. The gospel reading didn't lend itself to easy answers. It's about a Syro-phoenician woman who comes to Jesus seeking healing for her young daughter. And Jesus has a bad day, telling her "it is not right to take the children's bread and toss it to the dogs" (an ethnic slur). The woman doesn't back down, reminding Jesus that even the "dogs" eat the children's crumbs. And invites us all to a paradigm shift. A different way of seeing. A different way of being. A different way of loving.

The majority of us seem wedded to the notion of "fixing," and have an aversion to anything "broken" (especially our own brokenness). Which means that we make premature judgments, naming whatever is wounded or shattered or broken as wrecked or ruined, and we miss, we do not see, the flame and the glow that is within each and every one of us.

Nice and tidy is so tempting. The rabbi's invitation to dance, his gentle reminder to the congregation...A different way of seeing. A different way of being...That regardless of our confusion or conflict or messiness, we are not lost. There is inside of each of us, a dancer.

An invitation to epiphanies and openness and the sacred ordinary and walking and welcoming...

Can you tell me the last time you were invited—given the permission, just like the members of the synagogue—to be vulnerable, curious, lighthearted, inquisitive, spontaneous, intuitive, and playful?

To be filled with wonderment and laughter?

To dance with manatees?

To embrace the sacrament of the present moment?

What would that look like?

And if I invited you today, would you say yes?

Notes

1. Adapted from Ira Glass, *This American Life*, "Seemed Like a Good Idea at the Time," January 13, 2006.

2. Simone Weil, *Gravity and Grace*, translated by Emma Crawford and Marion von der Ruhr, (New York: Routledge, 2002), 150.

3. Adapted from Paul Krugman, "Death Comes Knocking," *The New York Times*, November 12, 2004.

4. Adapted from Gregory Boyle, *Tattoos on the Heart: The Power of Boundless Compassion* (New York: Free Press, 2010), 46.

5. Adapted from Jimmy Carter, *Our Endangered Values: America's Moral Crisis* (New York: Simon & Schuster, 2005), 27-28.

6. Adapted from by Claudia Herrera Hudson, Saint Francis of Assisi, myhero.com, 7/10/2015).

7. Adapted from Jack Wintz, OFM, "7 Key Moments in the Life of St. Francis," Franciscan Media (https://www.franciscanmedia.org/7-key-moments-in-the-life-of-saint-francis/).

8. Adapted from Margaret J. Wheatley, *Turning to One Another: Simple Conversations to Restore Hope to the Future* (San Francisco, Berrett-Koehler, 2009), 72.

9. Wayne Muller, *Sabbath: Finding Rest, Renewal, and Delight in Our Busy Lives* (New York: Bantam, 1999), 51.

10. Adapted from Eugene H. Peterson, *Christ Plays in Ten Thousand Places*, (Grand Rapids: Eerdmans, 2005), 69-70.

11. From Jon J. Muth, *The Three Questions*, based on a story by Leo Tolstoy (New York: Scholastic, 2002), 43-44.

12. Adapted from Rachel Naomi Remen, *My Grandfather's Blessings: Stories of Strength, Refuge, and Belonging* (New York: Riverhead, 2000).

13. Terry Hershey, *Soul Gardening: Cultivating the Good Life* (Minneapolis: Augsburg Fortress, 1999), 10-11.

14. Barbara Brown Taylor, *An Altar in the World: A Geography of Faith* (New York: HarperCollins, 2009), 15.

15. Desmond Tutu, Dalai Lama, Douglas Carlton Abrams, *The Book of Joy: Lasting Happiness in a Changing World* (New York: Avery, 2016),

16. Adapted from Tom Junod, "Can you say…Hero?", *Esquire Magazine*, November 1998)

17. Adapted from *The World's Fastest Indian*, Directed by Roger Donaldson. (New York: Magnolia Pictures, 2005).

18. Adapted from Scott Russell Sanders, *Hunting for Hope: A Father's Journeys*, (Boston: Beacon, 2000), 2-3.

19. Adapted from "Amid Violence in Baghdad, a Musician Creates a One-Man Vigil," National Public Radio, June 8, 2015.